Kitchen Treasury Series
FAMILY FAVORITES

Editorial Director
DONALD D. WOLF

Design and Layout
MARGOT L. WOLF

Published by
LEXICON PUBLICATIONS, INC.
387 Park Avenue South, New York, NY 10016

Cover illustration:
Veal Peasant Style 49

ISBN: 0-7172-4529-2

Contents

Appetizers

Daisy Canapés

MAKES 8
CANAPÉS

8 rounds bread
⅓ cup softened butter
1½ ounces anchovy paste
4 hard-cooked eggs

1. Spread untoasted rounds of bread with butter and then with anchovy paste.
2. Cut narrow strips out of hard-cooked egg whites.
3. Arrange in petal fashion on paste and place sieved hard-cooked egg yolk in center.

Wine-Cheese Canapés

ABOUT 24
CANAPÉS

½ cup whipped unsalted butter
4 teaspoons Roquefort cheese
4 toasted bread rounds
2 packages (3 ounces each) cream cheese
2 tablespoons sauterne
Parsley, minced
Pimento-stuffed olive slices
Paprika
Clear Glaze (below)

1. Whip together butter and Roquefort cheese. Spread onto toasted bread rounds.
2. Whip cream cheese with sauterne.
3. Pipe a swirl of the mixture onto each canapé. Roll edges in minced parsley. Top with pimento-stuffed olive slice; sprinkle.
4. Glaze and chill.

Clear Glaze: Soften **1 envelope unflavored gelatin** in ⅔ **cup cold water** in a bowl. Pour **1 cup boiling water** over softened gelatin and stir until gelatin is dissolved. Chill until slightly thickened. To glaze canapés: Place canapés on wire racks over a large shallow pan. Working quickly, spoon about 2 teaspoons of slightly thickened gelatin over each canapé. (Have ready a bowl of ice and water and a bowl of hot water. The gelatin may have to be set over one or the other during glazing to maintain the proper consistency.) The gelatin should cling slightly to canapés when spooned over them. Any drips may be scooped up and reused.

Cocktail Meatballs

30 to 40
MEATBALLS

1 large onion, minced
2 tablespoons olive oil
1½ pounds freshly ground round steak (half each of lamb and veal)
3 tablespoons cracker meal
2 cups firm-type bread, crust removed
2 eggs
6 tablespoons chopped parsley
2 teaspoons oregano, crushed
1½ teaspoons mint
2 tablespoons vinegar
Salt and pepper to taste
Flour
Olive or corn oil for deep frying heated to 365°F

1. Brown half of onion in 2 tablespoons oil in a small frying pan. Mix with the uncooked onion and add to meat in a large bowl. Add the remaining ingredients except flour and oil. Toss lightly with two forks to mix thoroughly.
2. Dust hands with flour. Roll a small amount of meat at a time between palms, shaping into a ball.
3. To heated fat in deep fryer, add the meatballs a layer at a time. Fry until browned on all sides (about 12 minutes). Serve hot.

Mushrooms à la Grecque

8 TO 10
HORS D'OEUVRE
PORTIONS

1 pound fresh mushrooms or
  2 cans (6 to 8 ounces each)
  whole mushrooms
⅓ cup olive oil
⅓ cup dry white wine or
  apple juice
¼ cup water
1 tablespoon lemon juice
¾ cup chopped onion
1 large clove garlic, minced
1½ teaspoons salt
1 teaspoon sugar
½ teaspoon coriander seed
  (optional)
¼ teaspoon black pepper
2 cups carrot chunks
½ cup pimento-stuffed olives

1. Rinse, pat dry, and halve fresh mushrooms or drain canned mushrooms; set aside.
2. In a large saucepan combine oil, wine, water, lemon juice, onion, garlic, salt, sugar, coriander, and black pepper. Bring to boiling; add carrots.
3. Cover and simmer for 15 minutes. Add mushrooms and olives. Return to boiling; reduce heat. Cover and simmer for 5 minutes.
4. Chill thoroughly, at least overnight.
5. To serve, thread mushrooms, carrot chunks, and olives on skewers or spoon into a bowl. Serve as hors d'oeuvres.

Mushroom Cheese Mold

3½ CUPS
SPREAD

2 packages (8 ounces each)
  cream cheese, softened
½ pound Cheddar cheese,
  shredded (about 2 cups)
1 clove garlic, crushed
1½ teaspoons brown
  mustard
¼ teaspoon salt
1 can (3 to 4 ounces)
  mushroom stems and
  pieces, drained and
  chopped
¼ cup finely chopped onion
2 tablespoons finely diced
  pimento
2 tablespoons finely chopped
  parsley
Sliced mushrooms (optional)
Parsley (optional)

1. Combine cheeses, garlic, mustard, and salt in a bowl. Add chopped mushrooms, onion, pimento, and parsley; mix well.
2. Turn mixture into a lightly buttered 3-cup mold. Refrigerate until firm.
3. Unmold onto serving platter. Garnish with sliced mushrooms and parsley, if desired. Serve with crackers.

Avocado Sandwiches on Sour Dough

8 SERVINGS

2 avocados, thinly sliced and
  salted
¼ cup butter (½ stick),
  softened
½ teaspoon oregano leaves
¼ teaspoon each chervil,
  parsley flakes, and grated
  lemon peel
Dash onion powder
8 slices sour dough or Italian
  bread, diagonally cut

1. Prepare avocado slices.
2. Cream butter with seasonings. Spread thinly over bread.
3. Top with avocado slices. Serve with white wine.

Feta Cheese Triangles

ABOUT
100 PIECES

1 pound feta cheese,
  crumbled
2 egg yolks
1 whole egg
3 tablespoons chopped
  parsley
Dash finely ground pepper
¾ pound butter, melted and
  kept warm
1 pound filo

1. Mash feta cheese with a fork. Add egg yolks, egg, parsley, and pepper.
2. Melt butter in a saucepan. Keep warm, but do not allow to brown.
3. Lay a sheet of filo on a large cutting board. Brush with melted butter. Cut into strips about 1½ to 2 inches wide. Place ½ teaspoon of the cheese mixture on each strip about 1 inch from base. Fold to form a triangle. Continue until all cheese mixture and filo have been used.
4. Place triangles, side by side, in a shallow roasting pan or baking sheet.*
5. Bake at 350°F about 20 minutes, or until golden brown. Serve at once.

Note: Feta cheese triangles freeze well. Before serving, remove from freezer and let stand 15 to 20 minutes. Bake at 325°F until golden brown.

*Pan must have four joined sides; otherwise butter will fall to bottom of the oven and burn.

Chili con Queso Dip

3¼ CUPS DIP

1 cup chopped onion
2 cans (4 ounces each) green
  chilies, chopped and
  drained
2 large cloves garlic, mashed
2 tablespoons cooking oil
1 pound process sharp Cheddar cheese, cut into chunks
1 teaspoon Worcestershire
  sauce
¼ teaspoon paprika
¼ teaspoon salt
½ cup tomato juice

1. Sauté onion, green chilies, and garlic in oil in cooking pan of chafing dish over medium heat until onion is tender.
2. Reduce heat to low, and add remaining ingredients, except tomato juice. Cook, stirring constantly, until cheese is melted.
3. Add tomato juice gradually until dip is the desired consistency. Place over hot water to keep warm.
4. Serve with **corn chips.**

Chicken Liver Spread

ABOUT
4 CUPS

½ pound chicken livers
1 cup milk
¼ cup rendered chicken fat
  or margarine
1 medium onion, cut in
  quarters
3 hard-cooked eggs, peeled
  and cut in half
½ pound cooked ham or
  cooked fresh pork, cut up
¼ teaspoon salt
¼ teaspoon pepper
⅛ teaspoon garlic powder
  (optional)

1. Soak livers in milk 2 hours. Drain livers and discard milk.
2. Melt fat in skillet. Add livers and onion and cook over medium heat until tender.
3. Combine livers, pan drippings, and all remaining ingredients. Grind or mince.
4. Add extra melted chicken fat or margarine, if desired, to make spread of desired spreading consistency.

Hot Crab Spread

2 CUPS

1 package (8 ounces) cream cheese, softened
1 tablespoon milk
2 teaspoons Worcestershire sauce
1 can (7½ ounces) Alaska King crab, drained and flaked, or 1 package (6 ounces) frozen crab meat, thawed, drained, and flaked
2 tablespoons chopped green onion
2 tablespoons toasted slivered almonds

1. Combine cream cheese, milk, Worcestershire sauce, crab, and green onion. Place in small individual casseroles. Sprinkle with almonds.
2. Bake, uncovered, at 350°F 15 minutes. Serve with **assorted crackers.**

Shrimp Dunk

25 TO 30 SHRIMP

1 can or bottle (12 ounces) beer plus ½ cup water
1 small onion, sliced
Top and leaves of 1 stalk celery
1 tablespoon salt
3 or 4 peppercorns
1 bay leaf
1 garlic clove
1 pound very large shelled shrimp, uncooked

1. Combine ingredients except shrimp in a large saucepan. Cover; heat to boiling. Boil 10 minutes.
2. Add shrimp. Cover and boil 5 minutes, or just until shrimp turn pink. Remove from heat; chill in cooking liquid.
3. Serve cold with dunking bowls of cold beer. Serve as hors d'oeuvres or as a summertime main entrée.

Eggplant Appetizer

ABOUT 4 CUPS

1 large eggplant
1 medium onion, minced
1 garlic clove, crushed in a garlic press
1 teaspoon chopped parsley
½ teaspoon freshly dried mint
½ cup olive oil
1 tablespoon wine vinegar (or more to taste)
Juice of 1 large lemon
Salt and pepper to taste

1. To prepare eggplant, place in a baking pan and prick top in four or five places with a fork.
2. Bake at 350°F about 45 minutes, or until skin is wrinkled and the surface is soft.
3. Cool eggplant slightly and cut in half. Scoop out the flesh and place in a blender. Add onion, garlic, parsley, and mint. Blend until well mixed.
4. Combine olive oil, vinegar, and lemon juice. Add to the eggplant mixture and blend well. Season with salt and pepper.
5. Chill. Serve with **toasted French** or **pita bread.** May also be used as a dip for fresh vegetables, or served separately as a first course.

Salads

Garden-Green Salad Mold

ABOUT
8 SERVINGS

1 package (3 ounces) lime-
  flavored gelatin
¼ teaspoon salt
1 cup boiling water
1 cup cold water
1 ripe medium avocado
1 tablespoon lemon juice
2 cups finely shredded
  cabbage
½ cup thinly sliced radishes
½ cup thinly sliced green
  onions with tops
Crisp greens

1. Put gelatin and salt into a bowl; add boiling water and stir until completely dissolved. Blend in cold water. Chill until slightly thickened.
2. Mash avocado and stir in lemon juice; blend thoroughly with gelatin. Mix in cabbage, radishes, and green onions.
3. Turn into a 1-quart mold or individual molds and chill until firm. Unmold onto chilled serving plate and garnish with salad greens.

Mixed Vegetable Salad

ABOUT
8 SERVINGS

1 cup diced cooked potatoes
1½ cups cooked sliced
  carrots
1½ cups cooked whole or cut
  green beans (fresh, frozen,
  or canned)
1½ cups cooked green peas
  (fresh, frozen, or canned)
1 cup sliced or diced cooked
  beets
Bottled Italian-style salad
  dressing
Lettuce
1 cup sliced celery
1 small onion, chopped
2 hard-cooked eggs, chopped
¾ cup small pimento-stuffed
  olives
¾ cup mayonnaise
¼ cup chili sauce
1 teaspoon lemon juice

1. Put potatoes, carrots, beans, peas, and beets into separate bowls. Pour salad dressing over each vegetable; chill thoroughly.
2. To serve, drain vegetables and arrange in a lettuce-lined salad bowl along with celery, onion, eggs, and olives.
3. Blend mayonnaise, chili sauce, and lemon juice. Pass with the salad.

Red Vegetable Salad

4 TO 6
SERVINGS

1 pint cherry tomatoes,
  stems removed, cut in half
20 radishes, sliced
1 small red onion, sliced
3 tablespoons wine vinegar
2 teaspoons salad oil
1 teaspoon salt
2 teaspoons snipped fresh
  mint
⅛ teaspoon freshly ground
  white pepper
Lettuce leaves

1. Combine all ingredients except lettuce leaves in a medium bowl; refrigerate covered 2 hours, stirring occasionally.
2. Serve vegetables on lettuce.

Vegetable Salad with Yogurt Dressing

4 SERVINGS

¾ cup Low-Fat Yogurt (below)
2 tablespoons snipped
  parsley
½ cup finely chopped dill
  pickle
½ cup chopped tomato
1 teaspoon salt
1 cup sliced radishes
1 medium zucchini, shredded
2 medium carrots, shredded
1 large beet, shredded

1. Mix yogurt, parsley, pickle, chopped tomato, and salt; refrigerate covered 1 hour.
2. Arrange radish slices around edge of a serving plate. Arrange zucchini, carrots, and beet decoratively in center of plate. Serve yogurt mixture with salad.

Low-Fat Yogurt

ABOUT
1 QUART

1 quart 2% milk
¼ cup instant nonfat
  dry-milk
2 tablespoons low-fat natural
  yogurt

1. Mix milk and dry-milk solids in a medium saucepan. Heat to scalding (150°F); cool to 110°F. Stir in yogurt.
2. Transfer mixture to a glass or crockery bowl. Cover with plastic wrap; wrap bowl securely in a heavy bath towel. Set in warm place (100° to 125°F)* for 4 to 6 hours, until yogurt has formed.
3. Place several layers of paper toweling directly on yogurt; refrigerate covered until cold.

*A gas oven with a pilot light will be about 125°F; however, use an oven thermometer, as temperature is very important. Turn an electric oven to as warm a setting as necessary to maintain temperature.
  Excess liquid and a coarse texture will result if temperature is too high. Liquid can be drained with a nylon baster. Blend yogurt in a food processor or blender to restore texture.

Note: This recipe can be made using skim or reconstituted dry milk, although the product will not be as rich.
  Purchased low-fat natural yogurt can be substituted in any recipe.

Molded Spinach Cottage Cheese on Platter

6 TO 8
SERVINGS

1 package (10 ounces) frozen
  chopped spinach
2 envelopes unflavored
  gelatin
¾ cup water
2 chicken bouillon cubes
2 tablespoons lemon juice
1½ cups creamed cottage
  cheese
½ cup sour cream
½ cup sliced celery
⅓ cup chopped green pepper
2 tablespoons minced green
  onion

1. Cook and drain spinach, reserving liquid. Add enough water to liquid to make ½ cup. Set spinach and liquid aside.
2. Soften gelatin in ¾ cup water in a saucepan; add bouillon cubes. Set over low heat; stirring occasionally, until gelatin and bouillon cubes are dissolved. Remove from heat; stir in spinach liquid and lemon juice. Set aside.
3. Beat cottage cheese until fairly smooth with mixer or in electric blender. Blend with sour cream and then gelatin mixture. Stir in spinach, celery, green pepper, and onion. Turn into a 5-cup mold. Chill until firm.
4. Unmold onto a chilled large platter. If desired, arrange slices of summer sausage around the mold.

Potato Salad

6 SERVINGS

½ cup olive oil
3 tablespoons wine vinegar
1 teaspoon oregano, crushed
2 tablespoons chopped parsley
1 medium onion, finely sliced
5 large red potatoes
Salt and pepper to taste

1. Combine olive oil, vinegar, oregano, parsley, and onion. Mix well. Set aside to marinate.
2. Scrub potatoes. Boil them in salted water in their jackets. When just tender (about 40 minutes), remove and plunge into cold water so they can be handled at once. Peel while hot and cut into even slices.
3. Pour the dressing over the potatoes; toss lightly. Add salt and pepper.

Tomato Aspic

6 TO 8 SERVINGS

4 cups tomato juice
⅓ cup chopped celery leaves
⅓ cup chopped onion
2½ tablespoons sugar
1¼ teaspoons salt
1 bay leaf
½ cup cold water
2 envelopes unflavored gelatin
2½ tablespoons cider vinegar

1. Set out a 1-quart mold.
2. Pour tomato juice into a saucepan.
3. Add celery leaves, onion, sugar, salt and bay leaf to tomato juice.
4. Simmer, uncovered 10 minutes, stirring occasionally.
5. Meanwhile, pour water into a small bowl.
6. Sprinkle gelatin evenly over water.
7. Let stand until softened.
8. Lightly oil the mold with salad or cooking oil (not olive oil); set aside to drain.
9. Remove tomato juice mixture from heat and strain into a large bowl. Immediately add the softened gelatin to hot tomato juice mixture and stir until gelatin is completely dissolved.
10. Add cider vinegar and stir well.
11. Pour tomato-juice mixture into the prepared mold. Cool; chill in refrigerator until firm.
12. Unmold onto chilled serving plate.

Salade Niçoise

6 TO 8 SERVINGS

Salad Dressing, below
3 medium-sized cooked potatoes, sliced
1 package (9 ounce) frozen green beans, cooked
1 clove garlic, cut in half
1 small head Boston lettuce
2 cans (6½ or 7 ounces each) tuna, drained
1 mild onion, quartered and thinly sliced
2 ripe tomatoes, cut in wedges
2 hard-cooked eggs, quartered
1 can (2 ounces) rolled anchovy fillets, drained
¾ cup pitted ripe olives
1 tablespoon capers

1. Pour enough salad dressing over warm potato slices and cooked beans (in separate bowls) to coat vegetables.
2. Before serving, rub the inside of a large shallow salad bowl with the cut surface of the garlic. Line the bowl or a large serving platter with the lettuce.
3. Unmold the tuna in center of bowl and separate into chunks.
4. Arrange separate mounds of the potatoes, green beans, onion, tomatoes, and hard-cooked eggs in colorful grouping around the tuna. Garnish with anchovies, olives, and capers.
5. Pour dressing over all before serving.

Salad Dressing: Combine in a jar or bottle ½ cup olive oil or salad oil, 2 tablespoons red wine vinegar, a mixture of 1 teaspoon salt, ½ teaspoon pepper, and 1 teaspoon dry mustard, 1 tablespoon finely chopped chives, and 1 tablespoon finely chopped parsley. Shake vigorously to blend well before pouring over salad.
ABOUT ⅔ CUP

Tossed Supper Salad

8 TO 10
SERVINGS

Dressing:
1 cup salad oil
½ cup cider vinegar
1 teaspoon salt
1 teaspoon sugar
½ teaspoon onion salt
¼ teaspoon crushed tarragon
¼ teaspoon paprika
¼ teaspoon dry mustard
¼ teaspoon celery salt
⅛ teaspoon garlic salt
⅛ teaspoon ground black
   pepper

Salad:
2 cans (6½ or 7 ounces each)
   tuna
½ head lettuce
1 cup spinach leaves, washed
1 cup diced celery
¾ cup chopped green pepper
½ cup cooked green peas
4 sweet pickles, chopped
4 radishes, thinly sliced
2 hard-cooked eggs, sliced
2 tablespoons chopped
   pimento
2 tomatoes, rinsed and cut in
   eighths
1 teaspoon salt
Tomato wedges
Ripe olives

1. For dressing, put oil and vinegar into a jar; mix salt, sugar, and seasonings; add to jar, cover, and shake well. Refrigerate until needed. Shake before using.
2. For salad, drain tuna well and separate into small chunks; put into a bowl. Toss tuna with ½ cup prepared dressing; cover and refrigerate 1 to 2 hours.
3. Tear lettuce and spinach into pieces and put into a large bowl. Add celery, green pepper, peas, pickles, radishes, eggs, and pimento; add the tuna with its dressing and tomatoes. Sprinkle with salt. Toss lightly until ingredients are mixed and lightly coated with dressing; add more dressing, if desired.
4. Garnish with tomato wedges and ripe olives.

Bacon-Bean Salad

ABOUT 12
SERVINGS

⅔ cup cider vinegar
¾ cup sugar
1 teaspoon salt
1 can (16 ounces) cut green
   beans
1 can (16 ounces) cut wax
   beans
1 can (16 ounces) kidney
   beans, thoroughly rinsed
   and drained
1 medium onion, quartered
   and finely sliced
1 medium green pepper,
   chopped
½ teaspoon freshly ground
   black pepper
⅓ cup salad oil
1 pound bacon, cut in 1-inch
   squares
Lettuce (optional)

1. Blend vinegar, sugar, and salt in a small saucepan. Heat until the sugar is dissolved and set aside.
2. Drain all beans and toss with onion, green pepper, vinegar mixture, and ground pepper. Pour oil over all and toss to coat evenly. Store in a covered container in refrigerator.
3. When ready to serve, fry bacon until crisp; drain on absorbent paper. Toss the bacon with bean mixture. If desired, serve the salad on crisp lettuce.

Note: If desired, omit bacon.

Rice Salad with Assorted Sausages

6 TO 8
SERVINGS

⅓ cup white wine vinegar
1 teaspoon lemon juice
¼ teaspoon French mustard
1 teaspoon salt
¼ teaspoon ground black
   pepper
⅓ cup salad oil
3 cups cooked enriched white
   rice, cooled
3 cups finely shredded red
   cabbage
½ cup raisins
½ cup walnut pieces
Greens
Link sausage (such as brat-
   wurst, smoky links, and
   frankfurters), cooked

1. Put vinegar into a bottle. Add lemon juice, mustard, salt, and pepper. Cover and shake. Add oil and shake well.
2. Combine rice, cabbage, raisins, and walnuts in a bowl; chill.
3. When ready to serve, shake dressing well and pour over salad; toss until well mixed.
4. Arrange greens on luncheon plates, spoon salad on greens, and accompany with assorted sausages.

Christmas Eve Salad

8 TO 10
SERVINGS

1 cup diced cooked beets
1 cup diced tart apple, not
   peeled
1 cup orange sections
1 cup sliced bananas
1 cup diced pineapple (fresh
   or canned)
Juice of 1 lime
Oil and Vinegar Dressing
Shredded lettuce
½ cup chopped peanuts
Seeds from 1 pomegranate

1. Drain beets well. Combine beets, apple, oranges, bananas, and pineapple. Refrigerate until ready to serve.
2. Add lime juice to beet-fruit mixture. Add desired amount of dressing and toss until evenly mixed and coated with dressing.
3. To serve, make a bed of shredded lettuce in salad bowl. Mound salad on top. Sprinkle with peanuts and pomegranate seeds.

Peach Wine Mold

ABOUT
8 SERVINGS

1 can (29 ounces) sliced
   peaches
1 package (6 ounces) lemon-
   flavored gelatin
1½ cups boiling water
1 cup white wine
⅓ cup sliced celery
⅓ cup slivered blanched
   almonds
Curly endive

1. Drain peaches thoroughly reserving 1¼ cups syrup. Reserve and refrigerate about 8 peach slices for garnish. Cut remaining peaches into pieces; set aside.
2. Pour gelatin into a bowl, add boiling water, and stir until gelatin is dissolved. Stir in reserved syrup and wine. Chill until partially set.
3. Mix peaches, celery, and almonds into gelatin. Turn into a 1½-quart fancy mold. Chill until firm.
4. Unmold salad onto a serving plate. Garnish with curly endive and reserved peach slices.

Blue Cheese Sour Cream Dressing

ABOUT
1½ CUPS
DRESSING

1 package blue cheese salad
   dressing mix
1 package (3 ounces) cream
   cheese, softened
1 cup sour cream

1. Prepare salad dressing following package directions.
2. Blend dressing with cream cheese in a bowl. Stir in sour cream until dressing is of desired consistency.
3. Serve dressing with **fruit and vegetable salad.**

French Dressing

ABOUT
1 CUP DRESSING

¾ cup salad oil or olive oil
¼ cup lemon juice or cider
  vinegar
1 tablespoon sugar
¾ teaspoon salt
¼ teaspoon paprika
¼ teaspoon dry mustard
¼ teaspoon pepper

1. Combine in a screw-top jar salad or olive oil, lemon juice or cider vinegar, sugar, salt, paprika, dry mustard and pepper.
2. Cover jar tightly and shake vigorously to blend well. Store in covered container in refrigerator.
3. Shake well before using.

Anchovy French Dressing: Follow recipe for French Dressing. Use lemon juice. Omit salt and add 4 minced **anchovy fillets.** Shake well.

Lorenzo French Dressing: Follow recipe for French Dressing. Add ¼ cup finely chopped **watercress** and 2 tablespoons **chili sauce.** Shake well.

Olive French Dressing: Follow recipe for French Dressing. Add ½ cup chopped **stuffed olives** and shake well.

Tangy French Dressing: Follow recipe for French Dressing. Add 3 to 4 tablespoons **prepared horseradish** and shake well.

Curried French Dressing: Follow recipe for French Dressing. Add ¼ teaspoon **curry powder** and shake well.

Fruit Juice French Dressing: Follow recipe for French Dressing. Substitute **orange** or **pineapple juice** for the lemon juice or vinegar, or use 2 tablespoons of each fruit juice.

Roquefort French Dressing: Follow recipe for French Dressing. Blend together until smooth 3 ounces (about ¾ cup) crumbled **Roquefort cheese** and 2 teaspoons **water.** Add dressing slowly to cheese, blending after each addition.

Honey-Lime French Dressing: Follow recipe for French Dressing. Substitute **lime juice** for the lemon juice or vinegar. Blend in ½ cup **honey** and ¼ teaspoon grated **lime peel.**

Vinaigrette French Dressing: Follow recipe for French Dressing. Add 2 tablespoons finely chopped **dill pickle,** 1 tablespoon chopped **chives,** and **1 hard-cooked egg** chopped. Shake well.

Tarragon French Dressing: Follow recipe for French Dressing. Use olive oil. Substitute **tarragon vinegar** for lemon juice or cider vinegar. Decrease sugar to 1 teaspoon. Add 1 clove **garlic,** cut into halves, ¼ teaspoon **Worcestershire sauce** and ⅛ teaspoon **thyme.** Shake well.

Italian Dressing: Follow recipe for French Dressing. Use olive oil. Omit lemon juice or vinegar and add 6 tablespoons **wine vinegar.** Reduce salt to ½ teaspoon. Omit sugar, paprika and dry mustard. Shake well.

Soups

Pioneer Potato Soup

4 TO 6
SERVINGS

1 quart chicken stock
4 potatoes, chopped (about 4 cups)
2 cups sliced carrots
½ cup sliced celery
¼ cup chopped onion
1 teaspoon salt
½ teaspoon marjoram, dill weed, or cumin
⅛ teaspoon white pepper
1 cup milk or half-and-half
2 tablespoons flour
Garnishes: paprika, sliced green onions, crisply cooked crumbled bacon, chopped pimento, snipped chives or parsley, or grated Parmesan cheese

1. Combine all ingredients except milk, flour, and garnishes in a large saucepan. Bring to boiling; simmer 30 minutes.
2. Gradually add milk to flour, stirring until smooth. Stir into soup.
3. Bring soup to boiling; boil 1 minute, stirring constantly.
4. Garnish as desired.

Potato Soup with Sour Cream: Follow recipe for Pioneer Potato Soup. Before serving, stir in **½ cup sour cream.** Heat; do not boil.

Pureed Potato Soup: Follow recipe for either Pioneer Potato or Potato Soup with Sour Cream, omitting the flour. Purée in an electric blender before serving. Reheat, if necessary.

Farm-Style Leek Soup

6 SERVINGS,
ABOUT
1½ CUPS EACH

2 large leeks (1 pound) with part of green tops, sliced
2 medium onions, sliced
1 large garlic clove, minced
¼ cup butter or margarine
4 cups chicken stock or bouillon
2 cups uncooked narrow or medium noodles (3 ounces)
1 can or bottle (12 ounces) beer
1½ cups shredded semisoft cheese (Muenster, brick, process, etc.)
Salt and pepper

1. Cook leek, onion, and garlic in butter for 15 minutes, using low heat and stirring often.
2. Add stock. Cover and simmer 30 minutes.
3. Add noodles. Cover and simmer 15 minutes, or until noodles are tender.
4. Add beer; heat to simmering. Gradually add cheese, cooking slowly and stirring until melted. Season to taste with salt and pepper.

Caraway-Cabbage Soup

12 CUPS;
8 TO 12
SERVINGS

3 tablespoons butter or margarine
1 head (2 pounds) cabbage, coarsely chopped
5 cups chicken stock
1 teaspoon caraway seed
¼ teaspoon pepper
1 can or bottle (12 ounces) beer
⅓ cup flour
1 cup cream, half-and-half, or milk
Salt

1. Melt butter; add cabbage. Cook slowly, stirring often, until limp.
2. Add stock, caraway seed, and pepper. Cover and simmer about 1 hour, adding beer during last 10 minutes.
3. Mix flour and a little cream to a smooth paste; add remaining cream. Stir into soup. Cook, stirring constantly, until bubbly and slightly thickened. Season to taste with salt.

Chinese Cabbage Soup

6 SERVINGS

2 cups cooked chicken, cut into strips (about 1 chicken breast)
7 cups chicken broth
6 cups sliced Chinese cabbage (celery cabbage)
1 teaspoon soy sauce
1 teaspoon salt
¼ teaspoon pepper

Combine chicken and chicken broth; bring to boiling. Stir in remaining ingredients; cook only 3 to 4 minutes, or just until cabbage is crisp-tender. (Do not overcook.)

Note: If desired, lettuce may be substituted for the Chinese cabbage. Reduce cooking time to 1 minute.

Brussels Sprout Soup

ABOUT
20 SERVINGS

4 packages (10 ounces each) frozen Brussels sprouts
7 bouillon cubes
5 cups boiling water
8 slices bacon, diced
2 cloves garlic, minced
6 cups milk
¾ cup uncooked rice
1 teaspoon oregano leaves, crushed
2 teaspoons salt
½ teaspoon pepper
1 package (10 ounces) frozen peas and carrots
1 teaspoon salt
2 cups water
¾ cup shredded Parmesan cheese
Assorted crackers

1. Set out a large saucepot or Dutch oven and a saucepan.
2. Partially thaw frozen Brussels sprouts.
3. Make chicken broth by dissolving bouillon cubes in boiling water. Set aside.
4. Fry in saucepot or Dutch oven the bacon and garlic.
5. Add 3 cups of the broth to saucepot with milk, uncooked rice, and a mixture of oregano leaves, salt and pepper.
6. Bring to boiling, reduce heat and simmer covered 15 minutes.
7. Add to saucepot the frozen peas and carrots. Bring to boiling, reduce heat and simmer about 10 minutes, or until vegetables are tender.
8. Meanwhile, coarsely chop the partially thawed Brussels sprouts. Combine in saucepan the remaining 2 cups of broth, salt and 2 cups water.
9. Bring to boiling and add the chopped Brussels sprouts. Return to boiling and simmer uncovered 10 minutes, or until tender.
10. Add Brussels sprouts with their cooking liquid to rice mixture. Stir in shredded Parmesan cheese. Accompany with assorted crackers.

Lettuce Soup

ABOUT
3 SERVINGS

2 tablespoons butter or margarine
2 tablespoons flour
1 can (about 10 ounces) condensed chicken broth
1 soup can water
½ small head lettuce, cored and coarsely chopped
¼ cup thinly sliced celery
1 tablespoon chopped watercress
Salt and pepper

1. Melt butter in a saucepot; stir in flour and cook until bubbly.
2. Gradually stir in chicken broth and water; bring to boiling, stirring constantly. Cook 1 minute.
3. Stir in lettuce, celery, and watercress. Season with salt and pepper to taste. Cook until vegetables are crisp-tender, about 5 minutes.

Blue Cheese Sour Cream Dressing

Beef Barley Soup

8 TO 10
SERVINGS

2 quarts water
1 soup bone with meat
½ cup chopped celery tops
1 tablespoon salt
½ teaspoon pepper
½ cup uncooked regular barley
3 cups coarsely chopped cabbage
1 cup sliced carrots
1 cup sliced celery
2 cups sliced parsnips
2 cups thinly sliced onion
1 can (12 ounces) tomato paste

1. Combine water, bone, celery tops, salt, and pepper in a Dutch oven. Bring to boiling; cover tightly and simmer 1 to 2 hours.
2. Remove bone from stock; cool. Remove meat from bone; chop. Return to stock.
3. Stir in barley; continue cooking 30 minutes.
4. Add remaining ingredients; simmer 30 minutes, or until vegetables are tender.

Meat Broth

ABOUT
1½ QUARTS

2 pounds beef shank or short ribs, or pork neckbones
1 pound marrow bones
3 quarts water
1 large onion, quartered
2 leaves cabbage
2 sprigs fresh parsley or 1 tablespoon dried parsley flakes
1 carrot, cut up
1 parsnip, cut up
1 stalk celery, cut up
5 peppercorns
1 tablespoon salt

1. Combine beef, bones, and water in a 6-quart kettle. Bring to boiling. Boil 15 minutes, skimming frequently.
2. Add remaining ingredients. Simmer rapidly about 1½ hours, or until meat is tender.
3. Strain off broth. Chill quickly. Skim off fat.
4. Remove meat from bones. Set meat aside for use in other dishes. Discard bones, vegetables, and peppercorns.
5. Return skimmed broth to kettle. Boil rapidly about 15 minutes, or until reduced to about 6 cups. Store in refrigerator until needed.

Meat Stock: Prepare Meat Broth as directed. Chill. Lift off fat. Boil until reduced to 3 cups, about 45 minutes.

Yellow Pea Soup with Pork

ABOUT
2½ QUARTS
SOUP

¾ pound (about 1⅔ cups) yellow peas
2½ quarts cold water
1 1-pound piece smoked shoulder roll
3 quarts water
¾ cup coarsely chopped onion
1 teaspoon salt
1 teaspoon whole thyme
¼ teaspoon sugar

1. Rinse, sort (discarding imperfect peas) and put peas into a large saucepan.
2. Pour 2½ quarts cold water over the peas.
3. Cover and set peas aside to soak overnight.
4. The next day, set out shoulder roll.
5. Put the shoulder roll, water and onion into a large sauce pot.
6. Simmer 1½ to 2 hours, or until meat is tender.
7. Remove meat and set aside. Skim off fat from liquid, leaving about 2 tablespoons. Drain the peas and add to the broth with salt, whole thyme, and sugar.
8. Simmer 1½ to 2 hours, or until peas are tender. If necessary, skim off shells of peas as they come to the surface.
9. Serve soup with thin slices of the meat.

Beef Barley Soup

Ham-Bean Soup

ABOUT
4 QUARTS SOUP

2 quarts water
1 pound (about 2 cups) dried
    Great Northern or pea
    beans
3 tablespoons butter
2 cups finely chopped onion
½ cup finely chopped celery
2 teaspoons finely chopped
    garlic
3 cans (about 10 ounces
    each) condensed chicken
    broth
Water
1 ham shank (about 4
    pounds) or 2 ham hocks
    (about 1½ pounds)
1 can (about 16 ounces)
    tomatoes or 4 to 6 medium-
    sized firm ripe tomatoes,
    peeled and chopped
2 whole cloves
1 bay leaf
¼ teaspoon freshly ground
    black pepper
2 cups shredded Cheddar
    cheese (about 8 ounces)

1. Bring water to boiling in a 6-quart saucepot. Add beans gradually to water so that boiling continues. Boil 2 minutes. Remove from heat and set aside 1 hour.
2. Drain beans, reserving liquid. Return beans to saucepot along with 4 cups of cooking liquid.
3. Melt butter in a large skillet. Add onion, celery, and garlic; cook 5 minutes, stirring occasionally. Turn contents of skillet into saucepot.
4. Combine chicken broth with enough water to make 6 cups. Pour into saucepot.
5. Peel skin from ham shank and cut off excess fat. Add shank and skin to saucepot along with tomatoes, cloves, bay leaf, and pepper. Bring to boiling, reduce heat, and simmer 2 to 2½ hours, or until ham is tender.
6. Remove ham shank and skin; cool. Transfer soup to a large bowl; remove bay leaf and cloves. Cut meat into pieces and return to soup. Refrigerate, then skim off fat.
7. Transfer soup to saucepot and bring to simmer. Add cheese and stir until melted.

Note: Soup may be stored in the refrigerator and reheated, or cooled and poured into freezer containers and frozen. Thaw and reheat over low heat.

Black Bean Soup

ABOUT
2 QUARTS SOUP

1 pound dried black beans,
    washed
2 quarts boiling water
2 tablespoons salt
5 cloves garlic
1½ teaspoons cumin
    (comino)
1½ teaspoons oregano
2 tablespoons white vinegar
10 tablespoons olive oil
½ pound onions, peeled and
    chopped
½ pound green peppers,
    trimmed and chopped

1. Put beans into a large, heavy saucepot or Dutch oven and add boiling water; boil rapidly 2 minutes. Cover tightly, remove from heat, and set aside 1 hour. Add salt to beans and liquid; bring to boiling and simmer, covered, until beans are soft, about 2 hours.
2. Put the garlic, cumin, oregano, and vinegar into a mortar and crush to a paste.
3. Heat olive oil in a large skillet. Mix in onion and green pepper and fry until onion is browned, stirring occasionally. Thoroughly blend in the paste, then stir in the skillet mixture into the beans. Cook over low heat until ready to serve.
4. Meanwhile, mix a small portion of **cooked rice, minced onion, olive oil,** and **vinegar** in a bowl; set aside to marinate. Add a soup spoon of rice mixture to each serving of soup.

Lentil Soup

6 TO 8
SERVINGS

1 package (16 ounces) dried
    lentils
2 quarts water
½ cup olive oil
1 cup chopped celery
½ cup grated carrot
1 onion, quartered
1 tablespoon tomato paste
3 garlic cloves, peeled
2 bay leaves
Salt and pepper to taste
Vinegar

1. Rinse lentils several times. Drain.
2. In a kettle put lentils, water, olive oil, celery, carrot, onion, tomato paste, garlic, bay leaves, salt, and pepper. Bring to a boil. Reduce heat and simmer covered 2 hours. Adjust salt and pepper.
3. Serve with a cruet of vinegar.

Tomato-Lentil Soup

6 TO 8
SERVINGS

2 cups chopped carrots
1 cup chopped onion
1 cup sliced celery
2 tablespoons margarine,
melted
1 clove garlic, crushed
1¼ cups (½ pound) dried
lentils
2 quarts water
1 tablespoon salt
1 can (6 ounces) tomato
paste
¼ teaspoon crushed dill
weed or tarragon

1. Sauté carrots, onion, and celery in margarine in a large saucepan until tender.
2. Add garlic, lentils, water, and salt. Simmer 2 hours, or until lentils are tender.
3. Add tomato paste and dill weed; stir.

Egg and Lemon Soup

6 SERVINGS

1½ quarts chicken stock
(homemade or canned)
1½ cups uncooked parboiled
rice
1 whole egg
3 egg yolks
Juice of 2 lemons
Salt and pepper to taste

1. Heat stock in a saucepan. Add rice and simmer, covered, until tender (about 20 minutes).
2. Beat egg and yolks until light. Beating constantly, slowly add lemon juice.
3. Measure 2 cups hot chicken stock and add, tablespoon by tablespoon, to egg mixture, beating constantly to prevent curdling. Add this mixture to the remaining hot chicken stock with rice. Season with salt and pepper.
4. Serve at once.

Sherried Chicken Chowder

8 SERVINGS

10 cups water
1 broiler-fryer chicken
(about 2½ pounds)
1 carrot, coarsely chopped
1 stalk celery, coarsely
chopped
1 onion, halved
4 whole cloves
2 teaspoons salt
1 teaspoon crushed tarragon
1 bay leaf
½ cup uncooked barley or
rice
½ teaspoon curry powder
¼ cup dry sherry
1 cup half-and-half

1. Place water, chicken, carrot, celery, onion halves studded with cloves, salt, and tarragon in Dutch oven or saucepot. Bring to boiling; simmer 1 hour, or until chicken is tender.
2. Remove chicken; cool. Discard skin; remove meat from bones; chop.
3. Strain stock. Discard cloves and bay leaf. Reserve stock and vegetables. Skim fat from stock.
4. Purée vegetables and 1 cup stock in an electric blender.
5. Return stock to Dutch oven; bring to boiling. Stir in barley and puréed vegetables. Simmer 1 hour, or until barley is tender. Stir in chicken, curry, sherry, and half-and-half.

Frosty Cucumber Soup

4 SERVINGS

1 large cucumber, scored
with a fork
¼ teaspoon salt
Pinch white pepper
1½ cups yogurt
1¼ cups water
½ cup walnuts, ground in an
electric blender
2 cloves garlic, minced
Green food coloring
(optional)

1. Halve cucumber lengthwise and cut crosswise into very thin slices. Rub inside of a large bowl with cut surface of ½ clove garlic. Combine cucumber, salt, and pepper in bowl. Cover; chill.
2. Pour combined yogurt and water over chilled cucumber; mix well. If desired, tint with 1 or 2 drops of food coloring. Chill.
3. Combine walnuts and garlic; set aside for topping.
4. Ladle soup into bowls. Place soup bowls over larger bowls of crushed ice. Serve with walnut topping.

Avocado Yogurt Soup

4 TO 6
SERVINGS

1 cup avocado pulp (2 to 3
avocados, depending on
size)
⅔ cup unsweetened yogurt
⅔ cup beef stock, or
bouillon made with ⅔ cup
water and 1 bouillon cube,
then chilled
1 tablespoon lemon juice
1 teaspoon onion juice or
grated onion
½ teaspoon salt
Dash Tabasco

1. Put avocado pulp and yogurt into an electric blender and blend until evenly mixed. Adding gradually, blend in beef stock, lemon juice, onion juice, salt, and Tabasco. Chill well.
2. Serve soup in chilled bowls.

Gazpacho Garden Soup

6 SERVINGS

3 large tomatoes, chopped
1 clove garlic, crushed
1 small cucumber, chopped
1 green pepper, chopped
½ cup sliced green onions
¼ cup chopped onion
¼ cup minced parsley
1 teaspoon crushed rosemary
¼ teaspoon crushed basil
½ teaspoon salt
¼ cup olive oil
¼ cup salad oil
2 tablespoons lemon juice
2 cups chicken broth or 3
chicken bouillon cubes
dissolved in 2 cups boiling
water, then cooled

1. Combine all ingredients except chicken broth in a large bowl. Toss gently.
2. Stir in chicken broth; chill.
3. Serve in chilled bowls with garnishes suggested in Gazpacho.

Pacific Seafood Chowder

ABOUT
8 SERVINGS

1½ pounds North Pacific
halibut, fresh or frozen
1 can (7½ ounces) Alaska
King crab or 1 package (6
ounces) frozen Alaska King
crab
3 medium potatoes
1 large sweet Spanish onion
¾ cup chopped celery
¼ cup chopped green pepper
2 cloves garlic, minced
¼ cup butter or margarine
2 cans (16 ounces each)
tomatoes
2 cups clam-tomato juice
1½ teaspoons salt
¼ teaspoon pepper
¼ teaspoon thyme
¼ teaspoon marjoram
1 dozen small hard-shell
clams
Snipped parsley

1. Defrost halibut, if frozen. Cut into 1-inch chunks. Drain canned crab and slice. Or defrost, drain, and slice frozen crab. Pare potatoes and cut into ½-inch pieces. Peel and thinly slice onion.
2. Sauté onion, celery, green pepper, and garlic in butter in a saucepot. Add tomatoes with liquid, clam-tomato juice, and seasonings. Cover and simmer 30 minutes. Add halibut, potatoes, and clams. Cover and simmer about 10 minutes, or until halibut and potatoes are done and clam shells open. Add crab and heat through.
3. Sprinkle with parsley. Serve with buttered crusty bread.

Rock Lobster Bouillabaisse

6 SERVINGS

¼ cup olive oil
1 cup chopped celery
1 onion, chopped
1 clove garlic, chopped
½ teaspoon thyme
1 bay leaf
1 can (28 ounces) tomatoes (undrained)
1 bottle (8 ounces) clam juice
1 cup dry white wine
¼ cup chopped parsley
1½ pounds fish fillets (turbot, flounder, cod, or halibut), cut in 2-inch pieces
1 pound frozen South African rock lobster tails
Salt and pepper

1. Heat olive oil in a saucepot and sauté celery, onion, and garlic until tender but not brown. Add thyme, bay leaf, tomatoes, clam juice, wine, and parsley. Cover and simmer 15 minutes.
2. Add fish to saucepot. Cut each frozen rock lobster tail into 3 pieces, crosswise through hard shell, and add to stew. Simmer 10 minutes.
3. Season to taste with salt and pepper. Remove bay leaf.
4. Ladle into large bowls and serve with slices of **French bread.**

Zuppa di Pesce: Royal Danieli

ABOUT
2½ QUARTS
SOUP

3 pounds skinned and boned fish (haddock, trout, cod, salmon, and red snapper)
1 lobster (about 1 pound)
1 pound shrimp with shells
1 quart water
½ cup coarsely cut onion
1 stalk celery with leaves, coarsely cut
2 tablespoons cider vinegar
2 teaspoons salt
¼ cup olive oil
2 cloves garlic, minced
1 bay leaf, crumbled
1 teaspoon basil
½ teaspoon thyme
2 tablespoons minced parsley
½ to 1 cup dry white wine
½ cup chopped peeled tomatoes
8 shreds saffron
1 teaspoon salt
½ teaspoon freshly ground black pepper
6 slices French bread
¼ cup olive oil

1. Reserve heads and tails of fish. Cut fish into bite-size pieces.
2. In a saucepot or kettle, boil lobster and shrimp 5 minutes in water with onion, celery, vinegar, and 2 teaspoons salt.
3. Remove and shell lobster and shrimp; devein shrimp. Cut lobster into bite-size pieces. Set lobster and shrimp aside.
4. Return shells to the broth and add heads and tails of fish. Simmer 20 minutes.
5. Strain broth, pour into saucepot, and set aside.
6. Sauté all of the fish in ¼ cup oil with garlic, bay leaf, basil, thyme, and parsley 5 minutes, stirring constantly.
7. Add to reserved broth along with wine, tomatoes, saffron, 1 teaspoon salt, and the pepper. Bring to boiling; cover and simmer 10 minutes, stirring occasionally.
8. Serve with slices of bread sautéed in the remaining ¼ cup olive oil.

French Onion Soup

6 SERVINGS

5 medium onions, sliced (4 cups)
3 tablespoons butter or margarine
1½ quarts beef broth
½ teaspoon salt
⅛ teaspoon pepper
Cheese Croutons (page 22)

1. Sauté onions in melted butter in a large saucepan. Cook slowly, stirring until golden (about 10 minutes).
2. Blend in beef broth, salt, and pepper. Bring to boiling, cover, and simmer 15 minutes.
3. Pour soup into warm soup bowls or crocks. Float a cheese crouton in each bowl of soup.

Cheese Croutons

6 slices French bread, toasted
2 tablespoons butter or margarine
¼ cup (1 ounce) grated Gruyère or Swiss cheese

1. Spread one side of each bread slice with butter. If necessary, cut bread to fit size of bowl. Sprinkle cheese over buttered toast.
2. Place under broiler until cheese melts.

Baked Minestrone

10 TO 12 SERVINGS

1½ pounds lean beef for stew, cut in 1-inch cubes
1 cup coarsely chopped onion
2 cloves garlic, crushed
1 teaspoon salt
¼ teaspoon pepper
2 tablespoons olive oil
3 cans (about 10 ounces each) condensed beef broth
2 soup cans water
1½ teaspoons herb seasoning
1 can (16 ounces) tomatoes (undrained)
1 can (15¼ ounces) kidney beans (undrained)
1½ cups thinly sliced carrots
1 cup small seashell macaroni
2 cups sliced zucchini
Grated Parmesan cheese

1. Mix beef, onion, garlic, salt, and pepper in a large saucepan. Add olive oil and stir to coat meat evenly.
2. Bake at 400°F 30 minutes, or until meat is browned, stirring occasionally.
3. Turn oven control to 350°F. Add broth, water, and seasonings; stir. Cover; cook 1 hour, or until meat is tender.
4. Stir in tomatoes, kidney beans, olives, carrots, and macaroni. Put sliced zucchini on top. Cover; bake 30 to 40 minutes, or until carrots are tender.
5. Serve with grated cheese.

Mulligatawny Soup

ABOUT 8 SERVINGS

1 broiler-fryer chicken (2½ to 3 pounds), cut in pieces
1 package soup greens (or see Note)
1 onion, peeled and quartered
1 teaspoon salt
1 bay leaf
1 cup water
5 thick slices lean bacon, diced
4 tomatoes, peeled and chopped
⅓ cup flour
2 teaspoons curry powder
Cayenne pepper
½ cup half-and-half

1. Put chicken, soup greens, onion, salt, bay leaf, and water into an electric cooker.
2. Cover and cook on Low 4 hours.
3. Remove chicken from cooker and set aside. Strain broth and reserve 1 cup. Pour remaining broth into cooker.
4. Fry bacon in a skillet until lightly browned. Add chopped tomato and cook 2 minutes. Stir in flour and curry powder. Add reserved chicken broth gradually, stirring constantly until mixture comes to boiling. Add to broth in cooker.
5. Remove chicken meat from skin and bones and cut in strips. Add to cooker; stir.
6. Cover and cook on High 2 hours.
7. Add cayenne and half-and-half to cooker; mix well.
8. Serve soup with **toasted bread cubes.**

Note: For soup greens, use all or a choice of the following vegetables: carrot, celery, leek, onion, parsnip, turnip; and herbs: parsley, tarragon, thyme.

Breads

Basic White Bread

5½ to 6 cups flour
2 packages active dry yeast
2 tablespoons sugar
2 teaspoons salt
1 cup milk
1 cup water
2 tablespoons oil
Oil or butter

QUICK MIX METHOD

1. Combine 2 cups flour, yeast, sugar, and salt in a large mixing bowl.
2. Heat milk, water, and 2 tablespoons oil in a saucepan over low heat until very warm (120° to 130°F).
3. Add liquid to flour mixture; beat on high speed of electric mixer until smooth, about 3 minutes. Gradually stir in more flour to make a soft dough.
4. Turn onto lightly floured surface and knead until smooth and elastic (5 to 10 minutes).
5. Cover dough with bowl or pan; let rest 20 minutes.
6. For two loaves, divide dough in half and roll out two 14x7-inch rectangles; for one loaf roll out to 16x8-inch rectangle.
7. Roll up from narrow side, pressing dough into roll at each turn. Press ends to seal and fold under loaf.
8. Place in 2 greased 8x4x2-inch loaf pans or 1 greased 9x5x3-inch loaf pan; brush with oil.
9. Let rise in warm place until double in bulk (30 to 45 minutes).
10. Bake at 400°F 35 to 40 minutes.
11. Remove from pans immediately and brush with oil; cool on wire rack.
ONE 2-POUND LOAF OR TWO 1-POUND LOAVES

CONVENTIONAL METHOD

1. Heat milk, sugar, oil, and salt; cool to lukewarm.
2. In a large bowl, sprinkle yeast in warm water (105° to 115°F); stir until dissolved.
3. Add lukewarm milk mixture and 2 cups flour; beat until smooth.
4. Beat in enough additional flour to make a stiff dough.
5. Turn out onto lightly floured surface; let rest 10 to 15 minutes. Knead until smooth and elastic (8 to 10 minutes).

6. Place in a greased bowl, turning to grease top. Cover; let rise in warm place until double in bulk (about 1 hour).
7. Punch down. Let rest 15 minutes.
8. Follow same shaping and baking instructions as Quick Mix Method.

You'll want to try these flavor variations to the Basic White Bread for something different. Shaping variations are also included.

Cheese Bread: Add **1 cup (4 ounces) shredded Cheddar cheese** before the last portion of the flour.

Onion Bread: Omit the salt and add **1 package (1⅜ ounces) dry onion soup mix** to the warm milk.

Mini Loaves: Divide dough into 10 equal pieces. Shape into loaves. Place in 10 greased 4½x2½x1½-inch loaf pans. Cover; let rise until double in bulk (about 20 minutes). Bake at 350°F 20 to 25 minutes.

Braided Egg Bread: Reduce milk to ½ cup. Add **2 eggs** with warm liquid to the flour mixture. Divide dough into 3 equal pieces. Form each into a rope, 15x12 inches. Braid. Tuck ends under. Place on a greased baking sheet or 9x5x3-inch loaf pan. Cover and let rise and bake the same as basic recipe.

French Bread: Omit the milk and oil and use **2 cups water.** Divide dough in half. Roll each half into 15x12-inch rectangle. Beginning at long side, roll up tightly. Seal seams. Taper the ends. With a sharp knife, make ¼-inch deep diagonal cuts along loaf tops. Cover. Let rise until less than double in bulk (about 20 minutes). Brush with water. Bake at 400°F 15 minutes, then reduce to 350°F and bake 15 to 20 minutes longer. For crisper crust, put pan of hot water in bottom of oven and 5 minutes before loaf is done, brush with glaze of **1 beaten egg white** and **1 tablespoon cold water.**

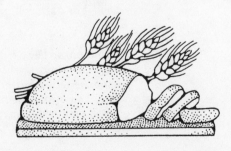

Delicatessen Rye Bread

2 LOAVES

2 to 2¾ cups all-purpose or
  unbleached flour
2 cups rye flour
2 teaspoons salt
2 packages active dry yeast
1 tablespoon caraway seed
1 cup milk
¾ cup water
2 tablespoons molasses
2 tablespoons oil

1. Combine 1¾ cups all-purpose flour, salt, yeast, and caraway seed in a large mixing bowl.
2. Heat milk, water, molasses, and oil in a saucepan over low heat until very warm (120° to 130°F).
3. Add liquid gradually to flour mixture, beating on high speed of electric mixer; scrape bowl occasionally. Add 1 cup rye flour, or enough to make a thick batter. Beat at high speed 2 minutes. Stir in remaining rye flour and enough all-purpose flour to make a soft dough.
4. Turn dough onto a floured surface; knead until smooth and elastic (about 5 minutes).
5. Cover with bowl or pan and let rest 20 minutes.
6. Divide in half. Shape into 2 round loaves; place on greased baking sheets. Cover; let rise until double in bulk (30 to 45 minutes).
7. Bake at 375°F 35 to 40 minutes, or until done.

Basic Dinner Rolls

2 TO 2½ DOZEN
ROLLS

4 to 4¾ cups all-purpose
  flour
2 tablespoons sugar
2 packages active dry yeast
1 teaspoon salt
1 cup milk
½ cup water
¼ cup butter or margarine
1 egg (at room temperature)
Melted butter (optional)

1. Combine 1½ cups flour, sugar, yeast, and salt in a mixing bowl.
2. Heat milk, water, and butter until very warm (120° to 130°F).
3. Add liquid and egg to flour mixture; beat until smooth, about 3 minutes.
4. Stir in enough remaining flour to make a soft, sticky dough.
5. Turn dough onto a floured surface; continue to work in flour until dough can be kneaded. Knead until smooth and elastic, but still soft (about 5 minutes).
6. Cover dough with bowl or pan. Let rest 20 minutes.
7. Shape dough as desired. Cover and let rise until double in bulk (about 15 minutes).
8. Bake at 425°F about 12 minutes. Cool on wire rack. Brush with butter if desired.

Pan Rolls: Divide dough into 24 equal pieces by first dividing dough in half and then each half into 12 equal pieces. Roll into balls. Place in a greased 13x9x2-inch baking pan. Brush with melted butter, if desired.

Cloverleaf Rolls: Pinch off bits of dough; roll into 1-inch balls. For each roll, place 3 balls in a greased muffin-pan well.

Crescents: Divide dough in half. Roll each half into a 12-inch round about ¼ inch thick. Brush with **2 tablespoons melted butter.** Cut into 12 wedges. For each crescent, roll up wedge beginning at side opposite the point. Place point-side down on a greased baking sheet; curve ends.

Snails: Roll dough into a rectangle ¼ inch thick. Cut off strips ½ inch wide and 5 inches long. Roll each piece of dough into a rope about 10 inches long. Wind into a flat coil, tucking ends under. Place on greased baking sheet.

Figure Eights: Shape strips of dough ½ inch wide and 5 inches long into 10-inch ropes as in Snails (above). For each roll, pinch ends of rope together and twist once to form a figure 8. Place on greased baking sheets.

Twists: Follow procedure for Figure Eights, giving each 8 an additional twist.

Bowknots: Roll dough into a rectangle ¼ inch thick. Cut off strips ½ inch wide and 5 inches long. Roll each strip into a smooth rope 9 or 10 inches long. Gently tie into a single or double knot. Place on a greased baking sheet.

Parker House Rolls: Roll dough ¼ inch thick. Brush with **3 or 4 tablespoons melted butter.** Cut with a 2½-inch round cutter. With a knife handle, make a crease across each circle slightly off center. Fold larger half over the smaller, pressing edges to seal. Place on a greased baking sheet or close together in a greased 13x9x2-inch baking pan.

Braids: Form several ropes, ½ inch in diameter. Braid 3 ropes into a long strip; cut into 3-inch strips. Pinch together at each end. Place on a greased baking sheet.

Butterflies: Divide dough in half. Roll each half into a 24x6-inch rectangle about ¼ inch thick. Brush with 2 **tablespoons melted butter.** Starting with long side, roll up dough as for jelly roll. Cut off 2-inch pieces. With handle of knife, press crosswise at center of each roll, forming a deep groove so spiral sides become visible. Place on a greased baking sheet.

Crusty Hard Rolls

1½ DOZEN ROLLS

3½ to 4½ cups all-purpose flour
2 packages active dry yeast
1 tablespoon sugar
1½ teaspoons salt
1 cup hot tap water (120° to 130°F)
2 tablespoons vegetable oil
1 egg white
1 egg yolk
1 tablespoon water

1. Combine 1 cup flour, yeast, sugar, and salt in a large mixer bowl. Stir in water, oil, and egg white; beat until smooth, about 3 minutes on high speed of electric mixer. Gradually stir in more flour to make a soft dough.
2. Turn dough onto a floured surface; knead until smooth and elastic (3 to 5 minutes).
3. Cover with bowl or pan and let rest about 20 minutes.
4. Divide into 18 equal pieces. Form each into a smooth oval; place on a greased baking sheet. Slash tops lengthwise about ¼ inch deep. Let rise until double in bulk (about 15 minutes).
5. Brush with a mixture of egg yolk and 1 tablespoon water.
6. Bake at 400°F 15 to 20 minutes. For a crisper crust, place a shallow pan of hot water on lowest oven rack during baking.

Sourdough Starter

2 cups flour
1 package active dry yeast
1 tablespoon sugar
2 cups warm potato water
  (105° to 115°)

1. Combine flour, yeast, and sugar in a nonmetal mixing bowl. Stir in potato water.
2. Cover; let stand in a warm place (80° to 85°F) for 48 hours.
3. Store in covered jar in refrigerator.

To use in recipe: Stir well before use. Pour out required amount called for in recipe and use as directed.

To replenish remaining starter: Mix in 1 cup each flour and warm water until smooth. Let stand in warm place a few hours until it bubbles again before covering and replacing in refrigerator.

Note: Use in recipe or remove 1 cup starter and replenish every week.

Sourdough Sam's Skillet Loaves

2 LOAVES

1 cup sourdough starter
2½ cups warm water
2 tablespoons honey or sugar
7 to 7½ cups all-purpose
  flour
¼ cup vegetable oil
1 tablespoon salt
1 teaspoon baking soda
6 tablespoons butter
4 tablespoons cornmeal

1. Combine starter, water, honey, and 5 cups flour in a large nonmetal mixing bowl. Cover with plastic wrap or a wet towel; let stand at room temperature 12 hours or overnight.
2. Stir in oil. Combine salt, soda, and 1 cup flour. Stir into dough; beat until smooth.
3. Stir in enough remaining flour to make a soft dough.
4. Turn dough onto a floured surface; continue to work in flour until dough is stiff enough to knead. Knead until smooth and elastic (about 5 minutes).
5. Divide dough in half. Roll each into a 10-inch round (see Note).
6. For each loaf, melt 3 tablespoons butter in a heavy 10-inch cast-iron skillet with heat-resistant handle. Sprinkle with 2 tablespoons cornmeal. Place dough in skillet. Turn over to coat top with butter and cornmeal. Let rise 15 minutes.
7. Bake at 400°F 25 to 30 minutes, or until done.
8. Serve hot with **butter** and **honey**.

Note: If you don't have 2 skillets, simply allow the second dough circle to rise while the first bakes – it will just have a lighter texture.

Sweet and Sourdough Granola Bread: Prepare dough as in Sourdough Sam's Skillet Loaves. After dividing dough in half, roll out each half into a 16x6-inch rectangle. Brush each with **2 tablespoons melted butter** and sprinkle with half the Granola Cinnamon Filling. Beginning with narrow end of rectangle, roll up tightly as for jelly roll; seal edges. Place loaves in 2 greased 9x5x3-inch loaf pans. Cover; let rise until double in bulk (45 to 60 minutes). Bake at 350°F 40 to 45 minutes.

Granola Cinnamon Filling: Combine **1 cup granola, ½**

cup firmly packed brown sugar, ½ cup chopped dates or raisins (optional), and 1 teaspoon cinnamon.

Sourdough Apple Kuchen: Prepare dough as in Sourdough Sam's Skillet Loaves. After dividing dough, roll out each half into a 10-inch round. Place dough in 2 greased 9- or 10-inch springform pans. Press dough about 1½ inches up sides of pan. Fill each kuchen with a mixture of 2 cups finely sliced pared apples, ½ cup firmly packed brown sugar, ¼ cup all-purpose flour, and 1 teaspoon cinnamon. Sprinkle with ¼ cup sliced almonds. Dot with 2 tablespoons butter. Let rise 30 minutes. Bake at 375°F 40 to 45 minutes, or until done.

San Francisco Sourdough French Bread

1 LOAF

1 cup sourdough starter
(page 26)
1½ cups warm water
2 tablespoons sugar
5 to 6 cups all-purpose flour
1 tablespoon salt
½ teaspoon baking soda

1. Combine starter, water, sugar, and 3 cups flour in a large nonmetal mixing bowl. Cover with plastic wrap or a towel; let stand at room temperature 12 hours or overnight.
2. Combine salt, soda, and 1 cup flour. Stir into dough; beat until smooth.
3. Stir in enough remaining flour to make a soft dough.
4. Turn dough onto a floured surface; continue to work in flour until dough is stiff enough to knead. Knead until smooth and elastic (5 to 8 minutes).
5. Shape dough into a long, narrow loaf by rolling and stretching dough as for French Bread (page #). Place on a greased baking sheet. Cover; let rise in a warm place until double in bulk (1½ to 2 hours).
6. With a sharp knife, slash top ½ inch deep at 2-inch intervals. Brush loaf with **water.**
7. Bake at 375°F 30 to 35 minutes.

Note: For a browner and shinier crust, brush before baking with a mixture of 1 egg white and ⅓ cup water instead of only water.

Peasant Black Bread

2 LOAVES

3½ cups rye flour
½ cup unsweetened cocoa
¼ cup sugar
3 tablespoons caraway seed
2 packages active dry yeast
1 tablespoon instant coffee
(powder or crystals)
2 teaspoons salt
2½ cups hot water (120°-
130°F)
¼ cup vinegar
¼ cup dark molasses
¼ cup vegetable oil or
melted butter
3½ to 4½ cups unbleached
or all-purpose flour

1. Thoroughly mix rye flour, cocoa, sugar, caraway, yeast, coffee, and salt in a large mixing bowl.
2. Stir in water, vinegar, molasses, and oil; beat until smooth.
3. Stir in enough unbleached flour to make a soft dough.
4. Turn onto a floured surface. Knead until smooth and elastic (about 5 minutes).
5. Place in an oiled bowl; turn to oil top of dough. Cover; let rise in warm place until doubled (about 1 hour).
6. Punch dough down. Divide in half; shape each half into a ball and place in center of 2 greased 8-inch round cake pans. Cover; let rise until double in bulk (about 1 hour).
7. Bake at 350°F 40 to 45 minutes, or until done.

Basic Sweet Dough

4 to 5 cups all-purpose flour
2 packages active dry yeast
1 teaspoon salt
¾ cup milk
½ cup water
½ cup melted butter
½ cup sugar
1 egg

1. Stir together 1¾ cups flour, yeast, and salt in a large mixer bowl.
2. Heat milk, water, butter, and sugar until very warm (120° to 130°F).
3. Add liquid ingredients to flour mixture; beat until smooth, about 2 minutes on electric mixer.
4. Add egg and ½ cup more flour and beat another 2 minutes.
5. Gradually add enough more flour to make a soft dough.
6. Turn out onto floured board; continue to work in flour until dough can be kneaded. Knead until smooth and elastic, but still soft (about 5 minutes).
7. Cover; let rest about 20 minutes.
8. Shape, let rise, and bake as directed in recipes that follow.

Cinnamon Rolls: Roll dough into a 13x9-inch rectangle. Spread with **2 tablespoons softened butter** or **margarine.** Sprinkle with mixture of **½ cup firmly packed brown** or **white sugar** and **2 teaspoons cinnamon.** Beginning with long side, roll dough up tightly jelly-roll fashion. Cut roll into 12 (1-inch) slices. Place slices in a greased 13x9x2-inch baking pan or greased muffin cups. Bake at 375°F 15 to 20 minutes.
1½ DOZEN

Glazed Raised Doughnuts: Follow recipe for Basic Sweet Dough. Roll out to about ½-inch thickness. Cut with doughnut cutter or make into shape of your choice, such as squares, twists, long johns, doughnut holes, or bismarcks. Let rise, uncovered, until light, 40 to 50 minutes. Fry in deep hot oil (375°F) 3 to 4 minutes, turning once. Drain on paper towels. Dip in a glaze of **1½ cups confectioners' sugar, 2 tablespoons warm water,** and **1 teaspoon vanilla extract.**

Apricot Crisscross Coffeecake: For one large coffeecake, roll dough into a 15x12-inch rectangle. For two small coffeecakes, divide dough in half. Roll each half into a 12x8-inch rectangle. Combine ½ **cup apricot preserves,** ½ **cup raisins,** and ½ **cup sliced almonds.** Spread half the filling lengthwise down the center of each rectangle. Make about 12 slashes, each 2 inches long, down the long sides of each coffeecake. Fold strips alternately over filling, herringbone fashion. Cover; let rise until double in bulk (50 to 60 minutes). Bake at 375°F 20 to 25 minutes for small coffeecakes and 35 to 40 minutes for large coffeecake.

Biscuits

ABOUT
1 DOZEN

2 cups all-purpose flour
1 tablespoon baking powder
1 teaspoon salt
⅓ cup butter or shortening
¾ cup milk

1. Combine flour, baking powder, and salt in a mixing bowl. Cut in butter with pastry blender or 2 knives until mixture resembles rice kernels.
2. Stir in milk with a fork just until mixture clings to itself.
3. Form dough into a ball and knead gently 8 to 10 times on lightly floured board. Gently roll dough ½ inch thick.

4. Cut with floured biscuit cutter or knife, using an even pressure to keep sides of biscuits straight.
5. Place on ungreased baking sheet, close together for soft-sided biscuits or 1 inch apart for crusty ones.
6. Bake at 450°F 10 to 15 minutes, or until golden brown.

Southern Buttermilk Biscuits: Follow recipe for Biscuits, substituting **buttermilk** for the milk and adding **¼ teaspoon baking soda** to the dry ingredients and reducing baking powder to 2 teaspoons.

Drop Biscuits: Follow recipe for Biscuits, increasing milk to 1 cup. Omit rolling-out instructions. Simply drop from a spoon onto a lightly greased baking sheet.

New England Blueberry Muffins

12 LARGE MUFFINS

1 cup sugar
½ cup softened butter or margarine
2 eggs
½ cup milk
2 cups all-purpose flour
2 teaspoons baking powder
½ teaspoon salt
1 to 1½ cups fresh or frozen blueberries

1. Combine sugar, butter, eggs, and milk in a mixing bowl; beat well.
2. Blend flour, baking powder, and salt; add and mix until blended (about 1 minute). Fold in blueberries.
3. Spoon into 12 well-greased muffin cups, filling almost to the top of the cup.
4. Bake at 375°F 20 to 25 minutes.

Irish Soda Bread with Currants

1 LARGE LOAF SODA BREAD

4 cups sifted all-purpose flour
2 tablespoons sugar
2 teaspoons baking soda
1½ teaspoons salt
¼ cup butter or margarine
⅔ cup dried currants, plumped
½ cup white vinegar
1 cup milk

1. Mix flour, sugar, baking soda, and salt in a bowl. Cut in the butter with pastry blender or two knives until particles resemble rice kernels. Lightly mix in currants.
2. Mix vinegar and milk. Add half of the liquid to dry ingredients; blend quickly. Add remaining liquid and stir only until blended.
3. Turn dough onto floured surface. Lightly knead dough about 10 times and shape into a round loaf.
4. Bake at 375°F 35 to 40 minutes.

Scones

1 DOZEN

1⅔ cups all-purpose flour
1 tablespoon sugar
1½ teaspoons baking powder
½ teaspoon baking soda
½ teaspoon salt
½ cup shortening
½ cup buttermilk

1. Combine flour, sugar, baking powder, baking soda, and salt in a mixing bowl. Cut in shortening with pastry blender or two knives until mixture resembles rice kernels.
2. Stir in buttermilk with a fork until mixture clings to itself.
3. Form dough into a ball and knead gently about 8 times on a floured surface. Divide dough in half; roll each into a round about ½ inch thick. Cut each round into 6 wedge-shaped pieces. Place on ungreased baking sheets.
4. Bake at 450°F 8 to 10 minutes. Serve warm.

Pasta and Grains

Polish Noodles and Cabbage

6 TO 8
SERVINGS

¼ cup butter or margarine
½ cup chopped onion
4 cups chopped or sliced
  cabbage
1 teaspoon caraway seed
½ teaspoon salt
⅛ teaspoon pepper
1 package (8 ounces) egg
  noodles
½ cup sour cream (optional)

1. Melt butter in a large skillet. Add onion; sauté until soft.
2. Add cabbage; sauté 5 minutes, or until crisp-tender. Stir in caraway seed, salt, and pepper.
3. Meanwhile, cook noodles in salted boiling water as directed on package. Drain well.
4. Stir noodles into cabbage. Add sour cream, if desired. Cook 5 minutes longer, stirring frequently.

Egg Noodles Abruzzi

4 TO 6
SERVINGS

1 tablespoon butter
¼ cup olive oil
1 pound ground lamb
2 green peppers, chopped
1 teaspoon salt
¼ teaspoon pepper
½ cup dry white wine
2 large tomatoes, peeled and
  coarsely chopped
1 pound egg noodles

1. Heat butter and oil in a large skillet. Stir in lamb and green peppers; season with salt and pepper. Brown the meat slightly, stirring occasionally.
2. Add wine and simmer until liquid is almost evaporated. Stir in tomatoes and simmer mixture 30 minutes, or until sauce is thick.
3. Cook noodles according to package directions; drain. Place noodles on a hot platter, pour sauce over noodles, and serve.

Fiesta Zucchini-Tomato Casserole

6 TO 8
SERVINGS

1½ quarts water
2 packets dry onion soup
  mix
4 ounces enriched spaghetti,
  broken
⅓ cup butter or margarine
⅔ cup coarsely chopped
  onion
1 cup green pepper strips
2 or 3 zucchini (about ¾
  pound), washed, ends
  trimmed, and zucchini cut
  in about ½-inch slices
4 medium tomatoes, peeled
  and cut in wedges
¼ cup snipped parsley
1 teaspoon seasoned salt
⅛ teaspoon ground black
  pepper
⅔ cup shredded Swiss cheese

1. Bring water to boiling in a saucepot. Add onion soup mix and spaghetti to the boiling water. Partially cover and boil gently about 10 minutes, or until spaghetti is tender. Drain and set spaghetti mixture aside; reserve liquid.*
2. Heat butter in a large heavy skillet. Add onion and green pepper and cook about 3 minutes, or until tender. Add zucchini; cover and cook 5 minutes. Stir in tomatoes, parsley, seasoned salt, and pepper. Cover and cook about 2 minutes, or just until heated.
3. Turn contents of skillet into a 2-quart casserole. Add drained spaghetti and toss gently to mix. Sprinkle cheese over top. If necessary to reheat mixture, set in a 350° oven until thoroughly heated before placing under broiler.
4. Set under broiler with top about 5 inches from heat until cheese is melted and lightly browned.

*The strained soup may be stored for future use as broth or for cooking vegetables, preparing gravy or sauce, as desired.

Spaghetti à la King Crab

ABOUT 6
SERVINGS

Parmesan Croutons
2 cans (7½ ounces each)
  Alaska king crab or 1
  pound frozen Alaska king
  crab
2 tablespoons olive oil
½ cup butter or margarine
4 cloves garlic, minced
1 bunch green onions, sliced
2 medium tomatoes, peeled
  and diced
½ cup chopped parsley
2 tablespoons lemon juice
¼ teaspoon thyme
½ teaspoon salt
1 pound enriched spaghetti

1. Prepare Parmesan Croutons; set aside.
2. Drain canned crab and slice. Or, defrost, drain, and slice frozen crab.
3. Heat olive oil, butter, and garlic in a saucepan. Add crab, green onions, tomatoes, parsley, lemon juice, basil, thyme, and salt. Heat gently 8 to 10 minutes.
4. Meanwhile, cook spaghetti following package directions; drain.
5. Toss spaghetti with king crab sauce. Top with Parmesan Croutons. Pass additional grated Parmesan cheese.

Parmesan Croutons: Put **3 tablespoons butter** into a shallow baking pan. Set in a 350°F oven until butter is melted. Slice **French bread** into small cubes to make about 1 cup. Toss with melted butter. Return to oven until golden (about 6 minutes). Sprinkle with **2 tablespoons grated Parmesan cheese** and toss.

Pasta with Fresh Tomatoes and Artichoke Hearts

For each serving:
1 medium ripe tomato,
  peeled, seeded, and diced
2 cooked artichoke hearts,
  cut in half
1 teaspoon oregano
½ teaspoon basil
1 garlic clove, crushed in a
  garlic press
Salt and pepper to taste
1 tablespoon wine vinegar
3 tablespoons olive oil
½ cup macaroni, cooked according to package
  directions
Mizithra cheese, cut in
  slices, for garnish
Kalamata olives for garnish

1. Combine all ingredients except macaroni and garnishes in a bowl. Cover and marinate several hours.
2. Turn macaroni onto a plate. Cover with marinated mixture. Garnish with cheese and olives. Serve cool.

Lasagne

6 TO 8
SERVINGS

Tomato Meat Sauce (see
  page 32)
3 tablespoons olive oil
1 pound ground beef
1 pound lasagne noodles,
  cooked and drained
¾ pound mozzarella cheese,
  thinly sliced
2 hard-cooked eggs, sliced
¼ cup grated Parmesan
  cheese
½ teaspoon pepper
1 cup ricotta

1. Prepare sauce, allowing 4½ hours for cooking.
2. Heat olive oil in a skillet. Add ground beef and cook until browned, separating into small pieces.
3. Spread ½ cup sauce in a 2-quart baking dish. Top with a layer of noodles and half the mozzarella cheese. Spread half the ground beef and half the egg slices on top. Sprinkle on half the Parmesan cheese and ¼ teaspoon pepper. Top with ½ cup ricotta.
4. Beginning with sauce, repeat layering, ending with ricotta. Top ricotta with ½ cup sauce. Arrange over this the remaining lasagne noodles. Top with more sauce.
5. Bake at 350°F about 30 minutes, or until mixture is bubbling. Let stand 5 to 10 minutes to set the layers. Cut in squares and serve topped with remaining sauce.

Tomato Meat Sauce

ABOUT
4 CUPS SAUCE

¼ cup olive oil
½ cup chopped onion
½ pound beef chuck
½ pound pork shoulder
7 cups canned tomatoes with liquid, sieved
1 tablespoon salt
1 bay leaf
1 can (6 ounces) tomato paste

1. Heat the olive oil in a saucepot. Add onion and cook until lightly browned. Put the meat into saucepot and brown on all sides. Stir in tomatoes and salt. Add bay leaf. Cover; simmer about 2½ hours.
2. Mix tomato paste into sauce. Simmer, uncovered, stirring occasionally, about 2 hours, or until thickened. If sauce becomes too thick, add ½ **cup water.**
3. Remove meat and bay leaf from sauce. Serve sauce over **cooked spaghetti.**

Tomato Sauce with Ground Meat: Follow recipe for Tomato Meat Sauce. When cooking is almost completed, brown ½ **pound ground beef** in **3 tablespoons olive oil,** cutting beef into small pieces with fork or spoon. After removing meat from sauce, add ground meat and simmer 10 minutes.

Tomato Sauce with Mushrooms: Follow recipe for Tomato Meat Sauce. When cooking is almost completed, lightly brown ½ **pound fresh mushrooms,** sliced, in **3 tablespoons melted butter.** After removing meat, add mushrooms and cook 10 minutes.

Tomato Sauce with Chicken Livers: Follow recipe for Tomato Meat Sauce. When cooking is almost completed, rinse and pat dry with absorbent paper ½ **pound chicken livers** and brown in **3 tablespoons olive oil.** After removing meat from sauce, and chicken livers and simmer 10 minutes.

Tomato Sauce with Sausage: Follow recipe for Tomato Meat Sauce. When cooking is almost completed, brown about ½ **pound Italian sausage,** cut in 2-inch pieces, in **1 tablespoon olive oil.** After removing meat from sauce, add sausage and simmer 10 minutes.

Fettuccine Alfredo

ABOUT
8 SERVINGS

1 pound green noodles
Boiling salted water
2 tablespoons olive oil
1 teaspoon chopped fresh basil
1 clove garlic, minced
Grated Parmesan cheese
Butter

1. Cook noodles in boiling salted water until just tender; drain.
2. In a chafing dish, heat olive oil, basil, and garlic. Toss the noodles in hot oil with a fork until they are very hot.
3. Sprinkle generously with Parmesan cheese, adding a generous piece of butter, and toss again a moment before serving.

Fettuccine al Burro Alfredo: Cook egg noodles in boiling salted water until barely tender, *al dente;* drain thoroughly. Bring quickly to the table in a heated serving bowl and rapidly toss and twirl with a generous amount of unsalted butter and finely grated Parmesan or Romano cheese so that the butter and cheese melt so quickly that the fettuccine can be served piping hot.

Ravioli

Tomato Meat Sauce (see
page 32)
3 cups (about 1½ pounds)
ricotta
1½ tablespoons chopped
parsley
2 eggs, well beaten
1 tablespoon grated
Parmesan cheese
¾ teaspoon salt
¼ teaspoon pepper
Basic Noodle Dough (see
page 34)
7 quarts water
2 tablespoons salt
Grated Parmesan or Romano
cheese

ABOUT
3 DOZEN
RAVIOLI

1. Prepare Tomato Meat Sauce.
2. Mix ricotta, parsley, eggs, 1 tablespoon grated Parmesan, ¾ teaspoon salt, and pepper.
3. Prepare noodle dough. Divide dough in fourths. Lightly roll each fourth ⅛ inch thick to form a rectangle. Cut dough lengthwise with pastry cutter into strips 5 inches wide. Put 2 teaspoons filling 1½ inches from narrow end in center of each strip. Continuing along strip, put 2 teaspoons filling at 3½-inch intervals.
4. Fold each strip in half lengthwise, covering mounds of filling. To seal, press the edges together with the tines of a fork. Press gently between mounds to form rectangles about 3½ inches long. Cut apart with a pastry cutter and press cut edges of rectangles with tines of fork to seal.
5. Bring water to boiling in a large saucepot. Add 2 tablespoons salt. Add ravioli gradually; cook about half of ravioli at one time. Boil, uncovered, about 20 minutes, or until tender. Remove with slotted spoon and drain. Put on a warm platter and top with Tomato Meat Sauce. Sprinkle with grated cheese.

Ravioli with Meat Filling: Follow recipe for Ravioli. Prepare sauce. Omit ricotta and parsley. Heat **2 tablespoons olive oil** in a skillet. Add **¾ pound ground beef** and cook until no pink color remains. Cook **½ pound spinach** until tender (see step 1 of Green Noodles, page #); drain. Mix spinach and ground beef with egg mixture. Proceed as directed.

Meat-Stuffed Manicotti

2 tablespoons olive oil
½ pound fresh spinach,
washed, dried, and finely
chopped
2 tablespoons chopped onion
½ teaspoon salt
½ teaspoon oregano
½ pound ground beef
2 tablespoons fine dry bread
crumbs
1 egg, slightly beaten
1 can (6 ounces) tomato
paste
8 manicotti shells (two thirds
of a 5½-ounce package),
cooked and drained
1½ tablespoons butter,
softened (optional)
1 to 2 tablespoons grated
Parmesan or Romano
cheese (optional)
Mozzarella cheese, shredded

4 SERVINGS

1. Heat olive oil in a skillet. Add spinach, onion, salt, oregano, and meat. Mix well, separating meat into small pieces. Cook, stirring frequently, until meat is no longer pink.
2. Set aside to cool slightly. Add bread crumbs, egg, and 2 tablespoons tomato paste; mix well. Stuff manicotti with mixture. Put side by side in a greased 2-quart baking dish. If desired, spread butter over stuffed manicotti and sprinkle with the grated cheese.
3. Spoon remaining tomato paste on top of the manicotti down the center of the dish. Sprinkle mozzarella cheese on top of tomato paste. Cover baking dish.
4. Bake at 425°F 12 to 15 minutes, or until mozzarella melts.

Eggplant Pugliese Style

Basic Noodle Dough

4 cups sifted all-purpose
  flour
½ teaspoon salt
4 eggs
6 tablespoons cold water

1. Mix flour and salt in a bowl; make a well in center, Add eggs, one at a time, mixing slightly after each addition. Add water gradually, mixing to make a stiff dough.
2. Turn dough onto a lightly floured surface and knead until smooth.
3. Proceed as directed in recipes.

Macaroni in Browned Butter with Grated Cheese

4 TO 6
SERVINGS

1 pound macaroni
1 cup butter
½ cup freshly grated
  kefalotyri or Parmesan
  cheese (or more to taste)

1. Cook macaroni according to directions on the package, adding ¼ **cup cooking oil** and **1 tablespoon salt**. Drain. Rinse under hot water.
2. Brown butter in a saucepan, stirring constantly.
3. Return the macaroni to the pot in which it was cooked, or place it in a warm serving dish. Drizzle the browned butter over it. With two spoons lift the macaroni to coat all the strands evenly. Cover with freshly grated kefalotyri. Serve at once.

Pasta with Beans Sorrento Style

4 TO 6
SERVINGS

2 cups dried Great Northern
  beans
5 cups water
1 teaspoon salt
1 cup chopped celery
1 cup chopped onion
3 tablespoons olive oil
1 teaspoon salt
6 ripe tomatoes, peeled and
  diced
1 tablespoon chopped Italian
  parsley
4 fresh basil leaves, chopped
  or 1 teaspoon dried basil
½ pound conchigliette

1. Rinse beans and put into a heavy saucepot or kettle. Add water and bring rapidly to boiling; boil 2 minutes and remove from heat. Cover; set aside 1 hour.
2. Stir 1 teaspoon salt into beans, cover, and bring to boiling. Cook until beans are nearly done, but still firm (about 2 hours). Drain and set aside.
3. Sauté the celery and onion in olive oil until soft. Sprinkle in 1 teaspoon salt, then stir in tomatoes, parsley, and basil.
4. Simmer 15 minutes, uncovered. Add the beans to tomato mixture; stir well. Cook the conchigliette according to package directions, drain, and stir into bean mixture. Serve in hot soup bowls.

Skillet Franks 'n' Noodles

4 TO 6
SERVINGS

1 pound frankfurters, cut in
  half diagonally
½ cup chopped onion
½ teaspoon basil or oregano
  leaves, crushed
2 tablespoons butter or
  margarine
1 can (10¾ ounces) con-
  densed cream of celery or
  mushroom soup
½ cup milk
½ cup chopped canned
  tomatoes
2 cups cooked wide noodles
2 tablespoons chopped
  parsley

1. In a skillet, brown frankfurters and cook onion with basil in butter until tender.
2. Stir in remaining ingredients. Heat, stirring occasionally.

Lemon Rice with Egg

ABOUT
4 SERVINGS

1¾ cups chicken broth
¾ cup uncooked long grain rice
1 egg
1 tablespoon lemon juice
¼ cup grated Parmesan cheese

1. Bring broth to boiling in a saucepan. Stir in rice; cover tightly. Cook 15 to 20 minutes, or until rice is tender and liquid is absorbed.
2. Place egg, lemon juice, and cheese in a bowl; beat until foamy. Stir into rice over low heat. Serve immediately.

Spinach with Rice

4 SERVINGS

1 medium onion, finely chopped
3 tablespoons olive oil
1 pound fresh spinach, washed well and drained, or 2 packages (10 ounces each) frozen leaf spinach, partially thawed
1 tablespoon tomato paste
¼ cup water
2 tablespoons long-grain rice
Salt and pepper to taste

1. In a saucepan, cook onion in olive oil until translucent. Add the spinach.
2. Mix tomato paste with the water and add along with rice; cover.
3. Simmer until rice is tender (about 20 minutes). Season with salt and pepper.

New Peas in Rice Ring

ABOUT
6 SERVINGS

1 package (6 or 6¾ ounces) seasoned wild and white rice mix
3 pounds fresh peas
Butter

1. Cook rice mix according to package directions.
2. Meanwhile, rinse and shell peas just before cooking to retain their delicate flavor. Cook covered in boiling salted water to cover for 15 to 20 minutes or until peas are tender. Drain and add just enough butter so peas glisten.
3. Butter a 1-quart ring mold. When rice is done, turn into the mold, packing down gently with spoon. Invert onto a warm serving platter and lift off mold.
4. Spoon hot peas into center of rice ring just before serving.

Cracked Wheat Pilaf

4 SERVINGS

3 tablespoons butter
1¼ cups cracked wheat
3 cups stock, heated
Salt and pepper to taste

Melt butter in a large saucepan, add wheat, and cook over low heat, tossing lightly with a fork until lightly browned. Add stock, cover, and simmer about 30 minutes until wheat is done. Season with salt and pepper.

Egg Barley

ABOUT
1 CUP DRY;
ABOUT
1¾ CUPS
COOKED

1 egg
3 tablespoons grated Parmesan cheese (optional)
Dash salt
1 cup all-purpose flour (about)

1. Beat egg with cheese (if desired) and salt, then add flour until a thick dough forms.
2. On a floured surface, knead in more flour until a stiff, dry dough forms.
3. Grate dough onto waxed paper. Let dry 1 to 2 hours.
4. Cook in **boiling soup** about 5 minutes, or until egg barley floats.

Vegetables

Stuffed Artichokes or Tomatoes

4 SERVINGS

4 cooked artichokes or 4
small tomatoes
¾ cup chopped onion
1 clove garlic, crushed
2 tablespoons butter
⅓ cup fine dry bread
crumbs
1 tablespoon chopped fresh
parsley
½ teaspoon dried basil leaves
½ teaspoon salt
¼ teaspoon pepper
1 tablespoon grated
Parmesan cheese (optional)
4 teaspoons butter or
margarine

1. Remove center leaves of artichokes; remove chokes. (Remove core from tomatoes and scoop out seeds; sprinkle inside with sugar and salt.)
2. Sauté onion and garlic in 2 tablespoons butter. Stir in bread crumbs, parsley, basil, salt, and pepper.
3. Fill vegetables with onion mixture. Sprinkle cheese on top. Set in a shallow casserole or baking dish. Place 1 teaspoon butter on top of each stuffed vegetable.
4. Bake at 375°F about 20 minutes, or until tender and browned on top.

Butter-Sauced Asparagus

ABOUT
6 SERVINGS

2 pounds fresh asparagus,
washed, or 2 packages (10
ounces each) frozen
asparagus spears, cooked
¼ cup butter
¼ cup chopped pecans
¼ cup finely chopped celery
1 tablespoon lemon juice

1. Put fresh asparagus into a small amount of boiling salted water in a skillet, bring to boiling, reduce heat, and cook 5 minutes, uncovered; cover and cook 10 minutes, or until just tender.
2. Meanwhile, heat butter in a small saucepan. Add pecans and celery and cook 5 minutes. Stir in lemon juice. Pour over asparagus and serve immediately.

Flavor-Rich Baked Beans

8 SERVINGS

1½ quarts water
1 pound dried navy beans,
rinsed
½ pound salt pork
½ cup chopped celery
½ cup chopped onion
1 teaspoon salt
¼ cup ketchup
¼ cup molasses
2 tablespoons brown sugar
1 teaspoon dry mustard
½ teaspoon ground black
pepper
¼ teaspoon ground ginger

1. Grease 8 individual casseroles having tight-fitting covers. (A 2-quart casserole with lid may be used.)
2. Heat water to boiling in a large heavy saucepan. Add beans gradually to water so that boiling continues. Boil 2 minutes. Remove from heat and set aside 1 hour.
3. Remove rind from salt pork and cut into 1-inch chunks; set aside.
4. Add pork chunks to beans with celery, onion, and salt; mix well. Cover tightly and bring mixture to boiling over high heat. Reduce and simmer 45 minutes, stirring once or twice. Drain beans, reserving liquid.
5. Put an equal amount of beans and salt pork chunks into each casserole.
6. Mix one cup of bean liquid, ketchup, molasses, brown sugar, dry mustard, pepper, and ginger in a saucepan. Bring to boiling. Pour an equal amount of sauce over beans in each casserole. Cover casseroles.

7. Bake at 300°F about 2½ hours. If necessary, add more reserved bean liquid to beans during baking. Remove covers and bake ½ hour longer.

Zesty Beets

ABOUT 4
SERVINGS

1 can or jar (16 ounces) small whole beets
2 tablespoons butter or margarine
2 tablespoons prepared horseradish
½ teaspoon prepared mustard
½ teaspoon seasoned salt

1. Heat beets in liquid; drain.
2. Add butter, horseradish, prepared mustard, and seasoned salt; stir gently.

Broccoli, Southern Style

ABOUT
6 SERVINGS

1 medium onion, thinly sliced
1 clove garlic, thinly sliced
2 tablespoons olive oil
1½ tablespoons flour
½ teaspoon salt
⅛ teaspoon pepper
1 cup chicken broth
4 anchovy fillets, chopped
½ cup sliced ripe olives
2 cups shredded process Cheddar cheese
2 pounds broccoli, cooked and drained

1. Cook onion and garlic in hot olive oil in a saucepan until onion is soft. Blend in a mixture of flour, salt, and pepper. Heat until bubbly.
2. Add chicken broth, stirring constantly. Bring to boiling and cook 1 or 2 minutes, or until sauce thickens.
3. Blend in anchovies, olives, and cheese. Pour sauce over hot broccoli.

Broccoli Florentine

4 SERVINGS

1 pound broccoli, washed and trimmed
2 tablespoons olive oil
2 cloves garlic, sliced thin
¼ teaspoon salt
¼ teaspoon pepper

1. Split the heavy broccoli stalks (over ½ inch thick) lengthwise through stalks up to flowerets. Put into a small amount of boiling salted water. Cook, uncovered, 5 minutes, then cover and cook 10 to 15 minutes, or until broccoli is just tender.
2. Meanwhile, heat oil and garlic in a large skillet until garlic is lightly browned.
3. Drain broccoli and add to skillet; turn to coat with oil. Cook about 10 minutes, stirring occasionally. Season with salt and pepper. Serve hot.

Broccoli Roman Style: Follow recipe for Broccoli Florentine. Omit cooking broccoli in boiling water. Cook broccoli in oil only 5 minutes. Add **1¼ cups dry red wine** to skillet. Cook, covered, over low heat about 20 minutes, or until broccoli is tender; stir occasionally.

Spinach Sauteed in Oil: Follow recipe for Broccoli Florentine; substitute **2 cups chopped cooked spinach** for broccoli. Add spinach, **1 tablespoon chopped pinenuts or almonds,** and **1 tablespoon raisins** to oil mixture.

Broccoli with Buttery Lemon Crunch

ABOUT
6 SERVINGS

1½ pounds broccoli, washed
¼ cup butter or margarine
½ cup coarse dry enriched bread crumbs
1 tablespoon grated lemon peel
3 tablespoons butter or margarine
1 small clove garlic, crushed in a garlic press or minced
½ teaspoon salt
Few grains black pepper

1. Cook broccoli in a small amount of boiling salted water until just tender. (Cook uncovered 5 minutes, then cover and cook 10 to 15 minutes, or cook, covered, the full time and lift the lid 3 or 4 times during cooking.)
2. Meanwhile, heat ¼ cup butter in a large skillet; add bread crumbs and heat, stirring frequently, until well browned. Remove crumbs from butter with a slotted spoon and mix with the lemon peel.
3. Put 3 tablespoons butter, garlic, salt, and pepper into skillet; heat until butter is lightly browned. Add broccoli and turn gently until well coated with butter.
4. Arrange broccoli in a heated vegetable dish and pour remaining garlic butter over it. Top with the "lemoned" crumbs.

Brussels Sprouts in Herb Butter

ABOUT
8 SERVINGS

2 pounds fresh Brussels sprouts
⅓ cup butter
1 tablespoon grated onion
1 tablespoon lemon juice
¾ teaspoon salt
¼ teaspoon thyme
¼ teaspoon marjoram
¼ teaspoon savory

1. Cook Brussels sprouts in boiling salted water until just tender.
2. Put butter, onion, lemon juice, salt, thyme, marjoram, and savory into a saucepan. Set over low heat until butter is melted, stirring to blend.
3. When Brussels sprouts are tender, drain thoroughly and turn into a warm serving dish. Pour the seasoned butter mixture over the Brussels sprouts and toss gently to coat sprouts evenly and thoroughly.

Brussels Sprouts and Grapes

4 TO 8
SERVINGS

1½ pounds fresh Brussels sprouts, cut in half
1½ cups beer
2 teaspoons clarified butter
¼ teaspoon salt
⅛ teaspoon freshly ground white pepper
1 cup seedless white grapes
Snipped parsley

1. Simmer Brussels sprouts in beer in covered saucepan until tender (about 8 minutes); drain.
2. Drizzle butter over sprouts; sprinkle with salt and pepper. Add grapes; heat thoroughly. Sprinkle with parsley.

Cabbage Casserole

SERVES 4

1 small head cabbage (1 pound)
2 carrots
1½ cups chicken stock or broth
5 peppercorns
1 (1 pound) can corn, drained
½ teaspoon salt
2 teaspoons soy sauce
4 hard-boiled eggs

1. Remove wilted leaves and cut the cabbage in strips. Pare the carrots and cut in slices.
2. Bring the chicken stock and peppercorns to a boil.
3. Add the cabbage and the carrots and boil, partially covered, for 15 minutes.
4. Add the corn and simmer until hot, about 5 minutes. Season with salt and soy sauce. Serve with egg halves. Garnish with chopped **parsley,** if desired.

Cabbage Rolls Paprikash

4 SERVINGS

8 large cabbage leaves
2½ cups diced cooked
  chicken
2 tablespoons chopped onion
½ cup finely chopped celery
¼ pound chopped fresh
  mushrooms
1 small clove garlic, minced
½ teaspoon salt
½ teaspoon thyme leaves
1 egg, beaten
2 tablespoons butter or
  margarine
6 tablespoons flour
2 cups chicken broth
2 cups sour cream
3 tablespoons paprika

1. Cook cabbage leaves 4 minutes in boiling salted water to cover. Drain and pat dry.
2. Mix chicken, onion, celery, mushrooms, garlic, salt, and thyme; stir in egg.
3. Place ½ cup of the chicken mixture in the center of each cabbage leaf. Fold sides of the cabbage leaf toward center, over filling, and then fold and overlap ends to make a small bundle. Fasten with wooden picks. Place in a 3-quart baking dish.
4. Heat butter in a large skillet. Blend in flour and heat until bubbly. Add chicken broth gradually, stirring until smooth. Blend in sour cream and paprika. Cook over low heat, stirring constantly, until thickened. Pour sauce over cabbage rolls. Cover baking dish.
5. Cook in a 350°F oven 35 minutes.

Danish Cabbage

6 SERVINGS

2 pounds cabbage
3 cups boiling water
1 cup sour cream
1 teaspoon caraway seed
½ teaspoon salt
½ teaspoon white pepper

1. Slice cabbage into small pieces and cook in boiling water covered 6 to 8 minutes until tender, but still crisp. Drain very well.
2. In the top of a double boiler toss cabbage with sour cream, caraway seed, salt and pepper. Cover and cook for 15 minutes.

Sweet-Sour Red Cabbage

6 SERVINGS

1 head (about 2 pounds) red
  cabbage
Boiling salted water to cover
  (1 teaspoon salt per quart
  of water)
½ cup firmly packed brown
  sugar
1 tablespoon caraway seed
½ cup vinegar
¼ cup butter

1. Set out a heavy 3-quart saucepan.
2. Remove and discard wilted outer leaves from red cabbage.
3. Rinse, cut into quarters (discarding core), and coarsely shred (about 2 quarts, shredded). Put cabbage into the saucepan and add water to cover, brown sugar, caraway seed.
4. Cook 8 to 12 minutes, or until cabbage is just tender. Remove from heat and drain.
5. Add to cabbage vinegar and butter.
6. Toss together lightly to mix.
7. Serve immediately.

Buttered Carrots

6 SERVINGS

1½ pound carrots
1 teaspoon sugar
½ teaspoon salt
⅛ teaspoon pepper
3 tablespoons butter
¾ cup water
1 tablespoon chopped parsley

1. Pare carrots and cut into julienne strips. Place in a large, heavy saucepan with sugar, salt, pepper, butter, and water. Cover.
2. Bring to boiling, then simmer 10 to 15 minutes, or until carrots are tender and moisture is evaporated. Remove cover to evaporate moisture, if necessary.
3. Turn carrots into a serving bowl and sprinkle with parsley.

Cauliflower with Mustard Sauce

4 SERVINGS

1 medium-size head
cauliflower
1 cup heavy cream
¼ cup sugar
2 tablespoons dry mustard
2 teaspoons cornstarch
½ teaspoon salt
1 egg yolk, slightly beaten
¼ cup cider vinegar

1. *For Cauliflower –* Remove leaves, cut off all the woody base and trim any blemishes from cauliflower.
2. Rinse and cook the cauliflower 20 to 25 minutes, or until tender but still firm.
3. *For Mustard Sauce –* Meanwhile, set out cream. Scald in top of double boiler ¾ cup of the cream.
4. Sift together into a small saucepan sugar, mustard, cornstarch, and salt.
5. Add, stirring well, the remaining ¼ cup cream. Gradually add the scalded cream; stir constantly. Stirring gently and constantly, bring cornstarch mixture rapidly to boiling over direct heat and cook for 3 minutes.
6. Wash double-boiler top to remove scum.
7. Pour mixture into double-boiler top and place over simmering water. Cover and cook 10 to 12 minutes, stirring occasionally. Remove cover and vigorously stir about 3 tablespoons of this hot mixture into egg yolk.
8. Immediately blend into mixture in double boiler. Cook over simmering water 3 to 5 minutes. Stir slowly to keep mixture cooking evenly. Remove from heat. Add gradually, stirring in vinegar.
9. Drain the cauliflower and serve on platter with **Schnitzel Holstein** or on a separate plate; pour the sauce over cauliflower.

Eggplant Pugliese Style

4 TO 6
SERVINGS

3 medium-size eggplants
(about ½ pound each)
2 tablespoons olive oil
1 tablespoon chopped parsley
1 medium onion, chopped
1 clove garlic, peeled and
chopped
1½ cups chopped cooked
meat (see Note)
½ cup fine dry bread
crumbs
1 tablespoon chopped
pinenuts or almonds
Salt and pepper
3 or 4 tablespoons olive oil
1 can (8 ounces) tomato
sauce

1. Wash and dry eggplants; remove stems. Cut eggplants in half crosswise, and scoop out most of the pulp; reserve pulp.
2. Heat 2 tablespoons olive oil in a skillet. Sauté pulp, parsley, onion, and garlic. Add meat, bread crumbs, and pinenuts. Season with salt and pepper; set aside.
3. Heat 3 or 4 tablespoons olive oil in another skillet. Cook eggplant shells in hot oil until the skins start to brown. Fill each half with the meat mixture. Pour tomato sauce over each half and cover skillet.
4. Cook eggplant slowly 20 to 30 minutes, or until tender.
5. If desired, place eggplant in a serving dish, add more tomato sauce, and keep in warm oven until ready to serve.

Note: If desired, ¾ pound uncooked chopped beef, lamb, or pork may be used. Sauté with pulp, parsley, onion, and garlic until browned before combining with other ingredients.

Crispy French Fried Onion Rings

2 sweet Spanish onions
1 cup pancake mix
¾ cup beer
Oil for deep frying heated to
 375°F
Salt

1. Peel onions and cut into ½-inch-thick slices; separate into rings.
2. Combine pancake mix and beer to make a smooth, thick batter.
3. Dip onion rings in batter and fry, a few at a time, in hot fat until golden brown. Drain on absorbent paper-lined baking sheets.
4. Keep fried onion rings hot in oven until all rings are fried.

Note: To freeze fried onion rings, leave onion rings on lined baking sheets, place in freezer, and freeze quickly. Then carefully remove rings to moisture-vaporproof containers with layers of absorbent paper between layers of onions. Cover container tightly and freeze. To heat frozen onion rings, place rings on a baking sheet and heat in a 375°F oven for several minutes.

Fresh Peas with Basil

ABOUT
4 SERVINGS

2 tablespoons butter or
 margarine
½ cup sliced green onion
 with tops
1½ cups shelled fresh peas
 (1½ pounds)
½ teaspoon sugar
½ teaspoon salt
⅛ teaspoon ground black
 pepper
¼ teaspoon basil
1 tablespoon snipped parsley
½ cup water

1. Heat butter in a skillet. Add green onions and cook 5 minutes, stirring occasionally. Add peas, sugar, salt, pepper, basil, parsley, and water.
2. Cook, covered, over medium heat 10 minutes, or until peas are tender.

Note: If desired, use 1 package (10 ounces) frozen green peas and decrease water to ¼ cup.

Stuffed Peppers

4 SERVINGS

4 green peppers
¼ cup olive oil
1 pound ground beef
1⅓ cups cooked rice
2 tablespoons minced onion
1 tablespoon minced parsley
½ teaspoon salt
¼ teaspoon pepper
1½ cups canned tomatoes,
 sieved
¼ cup water
¼ cup minced celery
1 tablespoon olive oil
½ teaspoon salt
¼ teaspoon pepper
Mozzarella cheese, cut in
 strips

1. Rinse peppers and cut a thin slice from stem end of each. Remove white fiber and seeds; rinse. Drop peppers into boiling salted water to cover and simmer 5 minutes. Remove peppers from water; invert and set aside to drain.
2. Heat ¼ cup oil in a skillet. Add ground beef and cook until browned. Stir in cooked rice, onion, parsley, ½ teaspoon salt, and ¼ teaspoon pepper. Lightly fill peppers with rice-meat mixture, heaping slightly. Set in a 2-quart baking dish.
3. Mix tomatoes, water, celery, and remaining oil, salt, and pepper; pour around peppers. Put strips of cheese on each pepper.
4. Bake at 350°F about 15 minutes.

Smothered Mixed Vegetables

8 small carrots, sliced
8 small potatoes
4 medium white turnips, pared and sliced
4 medium tomatoes, peeled, seeded, and quartered
2 small chayote or zucchini, sliced
1 green and 1 red sweet pepper, cut in strips
1 small eggplant (unpeeled), diced
Cauliflower chunks
½ cup green peas
½ cup lima beans
2 tablespoons peanut oil
1 large Spanish onion, sliced
1 cup stock or beef broth
¼ cup peanut oil
1 tablespoon salt
Freshly ground pepper
1 garlic clove, crushed in a garlic press
4 dried Italian pepper pods or 1 pink hot pepper
1 tablespoon tomato paste

1. Arrange in a top-of-range casserole with lid the sliced carrot, potatoes, turnip slices, tomato quarters, sliced chayote, pepper strips, diced eggplant, cauliflower chunks, peas, and beans.
2. Heat 2 tablespoons oil in a skillet over medium heat. Add onion and sauté until golden. Add stock, ¼ cup oil, salt, pepper, and garlic; pour over vegetables in casserole. Lay pepper pods over vegetables; cover and cook covered over low heat 45 minutes.
3. Remove cover, increase heat, and cook off most of the liquid. Remove peppers and stir tomato paste into vegetable mixture. Serve with **pepper steak** or well-browned **spareribs** or **pork chops.**

Parsley-Buttered New Potatoes

ABOUT
6 SERVINGS

18 small new potatoes
Boiling water
1½ teaspoons salt
2 tablespoons butter
1 tablespoon snipped parsley

1. Scrub potatoes and put into a saucepan.
2. Pour in boiling water to a 1-inch depth. Add salt; cover and cook about 15 minutes, or until tender. Drain and peel.
3. Return potatoes to saucepan and toss with butter and parsley.

Note: Snipped chives, grated lemon peel, and lemon juice may be used instead of parsley.

Hash Brown Potatoes au Gratin

ABOUT
6 SERVINGS

1 package (2 pounds) frozen chopped hash brown potatoes, partially defrosted
1½ teaspoons salt
Few grains pepper
¼ cup coarsely chopped green pepper
1 jar (2 ounces) sliced pimentos, drained and chopped
2 cups milk
¾ cup fine dry enriched bread crumbs
⅓ cup soft butter
⅔ cup shredded pasteurized process sharp American cheese

1. Turn potatoes into a buttered shallow 2-quart baking dish, separating into pieces. Sprinkle with salt and pepper. Add green pepper and pimentos; mix lightly. Pour milk over potatoes. Cover with aluminum foil.
2. Cook in a 350°F oven 1¼ hours, or until potatoes are fork-tender. Remove foil; stir potatoes gently. Mix bread crumbs, butter, and cheese. Spoon over top of potatoes. Return to oven and heat 15 minutes, or until cheese is melted.

Deviled Potatoes

SERVES 4

8 medium potatoes
½ teaspoon turmeric
1 teaspoon salt
1 teaspoon garlic powder
2 tablespoons vegetable oil
1 tablespoon chopped yellow
   onion
½ teaspoon freshly grated
   ginger
½ teaspoon chopped fresh
   chili pepper
⅓ cup boiling water
½ teaspoon crushed
   coriander seeds
½ teaspoon aniseed
½ teaspoon poppy seeds

1. Peel the potatoes and cut each lengthwise in 8 slices.
2. Mix turmeric, salt and garlic powder. Sprinkle this on the potatoes, stir and let stand for about 15 minutes.
3. Heat half the oil and fry the potatoes half soft on low heat.
4. Heat the rest of the oil in another pan and brown the chopped onion, the chili pepper and the ginger. Pour on the boiling water.
5. Add the potatoes and let them absorb the liquid over low heat.
6. Sprinkle on the other seasonings and shake the potatoes in the pan. Taste and correct seasoning with salt if needed.

Stuffed Baked Sweet Potatoes

4 SERVINGS

4 medium sweet potatoes,
   washed
1 small ripe banana, peeled
2 tablespoons butter or
   margarine
⅓ cup fresh orange juice
1 tablespoon brown sugar
1½ teaspoon salt
¼ cup chopped pecans

1. Bake sweet potatoes at 375° 45 minutes to 1 hour, or until tender when tested with a fork.
2. Cut a lengthwise slice from each potato. Scoop out sweet potatoes into a bowl; reserve shells. Mash banana with potatoes; add butter, orange juice, brown sugar, and salt and beat thoroughly. Spoon mixture into shells. Sprinkle with pecans. Set on a cookie sheet.
3. Return to oven 12 to 15 minutes, or until heated.

Spinach-Bacon Soufflé

6 SERVINGS

2 cups firmly packed, finely
   chopped fresh spinach
   leaves (dry the leaves
   before chopping)
¼ cup finely chopped green
   onions with tops
½ pound sliced bacon,
   cooked, drained and
   crumbled
3 tablespoons butter or
   margarine
¼ cup enriched all-purpose
   flour
½ teaspoon salt
¼ to ½ teaspoon thyme
1 cup milk
3 egg yolks, well beaten
4 egg whites
2 teaspoons shredded
   Parmesan cheese

1. Toss the spinach, green onions, and bacon together in a bowl; set aside.
2. Heat butter in a saucepan over low heat. Blend in flour, salt, and thyme. Stirring constantly, heat until bubbly. Add milk gradually, continuing to stir. Bring rapidly to boiling and boil 1 to 2 minutes, stirring constantly.
3. Remove from heat and blend spinach-bacon mixture into the sauce. Stir in the beaten egg yolks; set aside to cool.
4. Meanwhile, beat egg whites until rounded peaks are formed (peaks turn over slightly when beater is slowly lifted upright); do not overbeat.
5. Gently spread spinach-bacon mixture over the beaten egg whites. Carefully fold together until ingredients are just blended.
6. Turn mixture into an ungreased 2-quart soufflé dish (straight-side casserole); sprinkle top with Parmesan cheese.
7. Bake at 350°F 40 minutes, or until a knife comes out clean when inserted halfway between center and edge of soufflé and top is lightly browned. Serve immediately.

Green Tomatoes and Zucchini

6 TO 8
SERVINGS

2 tablespoons butter
1 large onion, chopped
¾ cup chopped, canned
   Mexican green tomatoes
   (tomatillos)
3 medium zucchini, thinly
   sliced
½ teaspoon oregano
½ teaspoon salt
1 tablespoon water
¼ cup grated Parmesan
   cheese

1. Heat butter in a large skillet. Add onion and cook until soft. Add green tomatoes, zucchini, oregano, salt, and water; stir. Cover; bring to boiling, reduce heat, and cook until zucchini is crisp-tender (5 to 7 minutes).
2. Stir in cheese just before serving.

Gingered Turnips

6 SERVINGS

2 pounds yellow turnips,
   pared and cubed
1 tablespoon minced onion
1¼ cups Beef Stock
½ teaspoon ground ginger
½ teaspoon sugar
2 teaspoons soy sauce

Combine all ingredients in a saucepan; simmer covered until turnips are tender (about 15 minutes). Drain; mash turnips with potato masher or electric mixer until fluffy; adding cooking liquid as needed for desired consistency.

Yams and Sweet Potatoes

Yams or sweet potatoes
Salt
Butter (optional)

Boil yams and serve plain sprinkled with salt and, if desired, topped with butter. Or barbecue yams on a grill 4 inches from ash-covered coals, turning frequently, until soft. Or bake yams until tender.

Zucchini Boats

6 SERVINGS

8 medium zucchini, washed
   and ends removed
1 medium tomato, cut in
   small pieces
¼ cup chopped salted
   almonds
1 tablespoon chopped
   parsley
1 teaspoon finely chopped
   onion
½ teaspoon seasoned salt
2 teaspoons butter, melted
¼ cup cracker crumbs

1. Cook zucchini in boiling salted water until crisp-tender, 7 to 10 minutes. Drain; cool.
2. Cut zucchini lengthwise into halves; scoop out and discard centers. Chop 2 shells coarsely; set remaining shells aside. Put chopped zucchini and tomato into a bowl. Add almonds, parsley, onion, and seasoned salt; mix well.
3. Spoon filling into zucchini shells. Mix butter and cracker crumbs. Sprinkle over filling. Set on a cookie sheet.
4. Place under broiler 4 inches from heat. Broil 3 minutes, or until crumbs are golden.

Meat

Roast Beef Filet with Burgundy Sauce

6 TO 8 SERVINGS

1 beef loin tenderloin roast,
  center cut (about 4 pounds)
Salt and pepper
½ cup dry red wine, such as
  burgundy
Sautéed mushroom caps
Parsley-buttered potatoes
Spiced crab apples

Burgundy Sauce:
½ cup warm water
¼ cup flour
1 cup beef broth
½ cup burgundy

1. Have butcher trim all but a thin layer of fat from meat and roll meat like a rib roast (but without adding fat).
2. Rub meat with salt and pepper and place in shallow roasting pan. Insert meat thermometer into center of thickest portion of roast.
3. Roast in a very hot oven, 450°F, about 45 to 60 minutes until thermometer registers 140°F (rare), basting twice with the wine after meat has cooked for 20 minutes.
4. Remove roast to heated serving platter. Garnish with sautéed mushroom caps, parsley-buttered potatoes, and spiced crab apples. Serve with Burgundy Sauce.
5. For sauce, pour off clear fat from drippings, saving ¼ cup.
6. Pour warm water into roasting pan; stir and scrape up all brown bits; strain.
7. Heat the reserved fat in a skillet; stir in flour. Slowly stir in strained liquid, beef broth, and burgundy. Cook and stir until sauce boils and thickens. Add a few drops of gravy coloring, if desired.

Bachelor's Steak

2 SERVINGS

2 small single-serving steaks
  (rib, rib eye, strip, T-bone)
1 garlic clove, halved
1 can (2 to 2½ ounces) sliced
  mushrooms
¼ to ⅓ cup beer
1 tablespoon flour
¼ teaspoon salt
Dash pepper

1. Rub meat with cut surface of garlic. Broil 2 to 3 inches from heat until as done as desired.
2. Meanwhile, drain mushroom liquid into measuring cup. Add enough beer to measure ⅔ cup total liquid.
3. Pour 2 tablespoons steak drippings into a saucepan; stir in flour, salt, and pepper until smooth. Stir in beer mixture. Cook, stirring constantly, until thickened and smooth. Add drained mushrooms; heat through.
4. Pour beer-mushroom sauce over steak and **potatoes.**

Swiss Steak Mozzarella

8 SERVINGS

2 pounds beef round steak,
  ½ inch thick
3 tablespoons flour
½ cup butter or margarine
1 can (16 ounces) tomatoes,
  cut up
1¼ teaspoons salt
¼ teaspoon basil
½ cup chopped green pepper
1½ cups (6 ounces) moz-
  zarella cheese

1. Cut meat into serving-size pieces; coat with flour.
2. Melt butter in a skillet. Brown meat slowly on both sides. Put into a 12x8-inch baking dish.
3. Combine tomatoes, salt, basil, and green pepper. Pour over meat.
4. Bake, covered, at 350°F 1 hour, or until meat is tender. Remove cover. Sprinkle with cheese and bake an additional 5 minutes, or until cheese is melted.

Savory Beef Stew

6 SERVINGS

1½ pounds beef stew meat, boneless, cut in 1½-inch cubes
¼ cup flour
1 teaspoon salt
¼ teaspoon basil
¼ teaspoon savory or marjoram
⅛ teaspoon pepper
3 tablespoons vegetable oil
2 onions, sliced
1 can or bottle (12 ounces) beer
½ cup water
1 bay leaf
5 medium potatoes (1⅔ pounds)
1 pound carrots (8 to 10); or ½ pound each parsnips and carrots

1. Dredge meat in mixture of flour, salt, basil, savory, and pepper. Reserve excess flour. Brown meat in oil. Add onion, beer, water, and bay leaf. Cover and simmer 1½ hours.
2. Pare potatoes; cut into large cubes. Slice carrots and/or parsnips. Add vegetables to stew. If necessary, add a little more water.
3. Cover and simmer 1 hour more, or until meat and vegetables are tender. Make smooth paste of reserved flour mixture and a little water. Stir into stew during last 10 minutes of cooking.

Oven Beef Bake

8 SERVINGS

2 pounds beef stew meat, cut in 1-inch cubes
1 can (10¾ ounces) condensed cream of mushroom soup
1 can (10½ ounces) condensed onion soup
¼ cup dry vermouth

1. Put meat into a 2-quart casserole.
2. Combine mushroom soup, onion soup, and vermouth. Pour over meat.
3. Bake, covered, at 325°F 3 hours, or until meat is tender. Serve with **hot, cooked noodles.**

Marinated Beef

8 TO 10 SERVINGS

4 pound blade pot roast of beef (any beef pot roast may be used)
2 cups vinegar
2 cups water
1 large onion, sliced
¼ cup sugar
2 teaspoons salt
10 peppercorns
3 whole cloves
2 bay leaves
1 lemon, rinsed and cut into ¼-inch slices
2 tablespoons butter
¼ cup butter
¼ cup all-purpose flour
3 cups liquid (reserved cooking liquid and enough reserved marinade or hot water to equal 3 cups liquid)
½ cup thick sour cream

1. Have ready 4-pound pot roast of beef. Put the meat into a deep 3- or 4-quart bowl. Set aside.
2. Combine in a saucepan and heat, without boiling, vinegar, water, onion, sugar, salt, peppercorns, cloves, and bay leaves.
3. Pour hot mixture over meat in bowl and allow to cool. Add lemon.
4. Cover and set in refrigerator. Marinate for 4 days, turning meat once each day.
5. Set out a heavy 4-quart kettle or Dutch oven and a tight-fitting cover.
6. Remove meat from marinade and drain thoroughly. Strain and reserve marinade.
7. Heat butter in the kettle over low heat.
8. Add the pot roast and brown slowly on all sides over medium heat. Slowly add 2 cups of the reserved marinade (reserve remaining marinade for gravy). Bring liquid to boiling. Reduce heat; cover kettle tightly and simmer 2½ to 3 hours., or until meat is tender when pierced with a fork. Add more of the marinade if necessary. Liquid surrounding meat should at all times be simmering, not boiling.

9. Remove meat to a warm platter and keep warm. Pour cooking liquid from kettle and set aside for gravy. For gravy melt butter in the kettle. Blend in ¼ cup of flour.

10. Heat until butter-flour mixture bubbles and is golden brown, stirring constantly. Remove kettle from heat.

11. Add liquid gradually, stirring constantly.

12. Return to heat. Bring to boiling; cook rapidly, stirring constantly, until gravy thickens. Cook 1 to 2 minutes longer. Remove from heat. Stirring vigorously with a French whip, whisk beater, or fork, add sour cream to kettle in very small amounts.

13. Cook mixture over low heat about 3 to 5 minutes stirring constantly, until thoroughly heated; do not boil. Serve meat and gravy with potato pancakes.

Beef Bourguignon

8 SERVINGS

¼ cup flour
1 teaspoon salt
½ teaspoon freshly ground black pepper
2 pounds beef stew meat, cut in 2-inch cubes
¼ cup butter or margarine
1 medium onion, chopped
2 medium carrots, chopped
1 garlic clove, minced
2 cups dry red wine
1 can (6 ounces) mushroom crowns, drained, reserving liquid
1 bay leaf
3 tablespoons snipped parsley
½ teaspoon thyme
1 can (16 ounces) onions, drained

1. Combine flour, salt, and pepper; coat beef cubes.

2. Brown beef in butter in a skillet. Pour into a 2-quart casserole.

3. Add onion, carrots, and garlic to skillet. Cook until tender but not brown. Add wine, liquid from mushrooms, bay leaf, parsley, and thyme. Pour over meat.

4. Bake, covered, at 350°F 2½ hours. Remove cover. Add onions and mushroom crowns. Bake an additional 30 minutes, or until meat is tender.

Beef Burgundy

6 TO 8 SERVINGS

2 slices bacon
2 pounds beef round tip steak, cut in 2-inch cubes
2 tablespoons flour
1 teaspoon seasoned salt
1 package beef stew seasoning mix
1 cup burgundy
1 cup water
1 tablespoon tomato paste
12 small boiling onions
4 ounces fresh mushrooms, sliced and lightly browned in 1 tablespoon butter or margarine
16 cherry tomatoes, stems removed

1. Fry bacon in a Dutch oven; remove bacon. Coat meat cubes with a blend of flour and seasoned salt. Add to fat in Dutch oven and brown thoroughly. Add beef stew seasonings mix, burgundy, water, and tomato paste. Cover and simmer gently 45 minutes.

2. Peel onions and pierce each end with a fork so they will retain their shape when cooked. Add onions to beef mixture and simmer 40 minutes, or until meat and onions are tender. Add mushrooms and cherry tomatoes; simmer 3 minutes. Pour into a serving dish.

Note: If cherry tomatoes are not available, use canned whole peeled tomatoes.

Pot Roast of Beef with Wine

8 TO 10
SERVINGS

3- to 4-pound beef pot roast, boneless (rump, chuck, or round)
2 cups red wine
2 medium onions, chopped
3 medium carrots, washed, pared, and sliced
1 clove garlic
1 bay leaf
¼ cup all-purpose flour
2 teaspoons salt
¼ teaspoon pepper
3 tablespoons butter
2 cups red wine
1 cup cold water
¼ cup all-purpose flour

1. Put the meat into a deep bowl. Add wine, onions, carrots, garlic, bay leaf, pepper. Cover and put into refrigerator to marinate 12 hours, or overnight; turn meat occasionally. Drain the meat, reserving marinade, and pat meat dry with absorbent paper.
2. Coat meat evenly with a mixture of flour, salt, and pepper.
3. Heat butter in a large saucepot; brown the meat slowly on all sides in the butter. Drain off the fat. Add the marinade and wine. Cover and bring to boiling. Reduce heat and simmer slowly 2½ to 3 hours, or until meat is tender.
4. Remove meat to a warm platter.
5. Strain the cooking liquid. Return the strained liquid to saucepot.
6. Pour water into a screw-top jar and add flour; cover jar tightly and shake until mixture is well blended.
7. Stirring constantly, slowly pour one half of the blended mixture into liquid in saucepot. Bring to boiling. Gradually add only what is needed of the remaining blended mixture for consistency desired. Bring gravy to boiling after each addition.
8. Serve meat with gravy.

Beef and Pea Casserole

6 SERVINGS

1 pound ground beef
1 medium onion, chopped
1 can (10¾ ounces) condensed tomato soup
⅓ cup water
2 cups cooked noodles
1 can (8 ounces) peas, drained*
1 can (4 ounces) sliced mushrooms, drained*

1. Brown ground beef and onion in a skillet; drain off excess fat. Combine with remaining ingredients. Put into a 2-quart casserole.
2. Bake, covered, at 350°F 30 minutes, or until heated through. To serve, sprinkle with **Parmesan cheese** and garnish with **pimento strips.**

*The liquid from the peas or mushrooms may be substituted for the ⅓ cup water.

Easy Corned Beef Bake

4 SERVINGS

½ package (6 ounces) noodles, cooked and drained
1 can (12 ounces) corned beef, cut up
1 cup (4 ounces) shredded American cheese
¾ cup milk
¼ cup chopped onion
½ cup fine dry bread crumbs
2 tablespoons butter or margarine

1. Combine noodles, corned beef, cheese, milk, and onion. Put into a greased 1½-quart casserole.
2. Top with bread crumbs. Dot with butter.
3. Bake, covered, at 325°F 45 minutes, or until casserole is bubbly.

Game Hens with Spicy Stuffing

Stuffed Veal Steak

4 SERVINGS

4 veal loin top loin chops, 1 inch thick (about 1½ pounds)
1 cup dry white wine, such as chablis
½ cup sliced mushrooms
1 green pepper, cut in ½-inch pieces
½ cup butter or margarine
½ cup all-purpose flour
1 egg, fork beaten
½ cup fine dry bread crumbs
½ cup grated Parmesan cheese
4 slices prosciutto (Italian ham)
4 slices (4 ounces) Cheddar cheese

1. Make a cut in the side of each veal chop, cutting almost all the way through. Lay each open and pound flat. Marinate meat for 1 hour in wine.
2. While meat marinates, sauté mushrooms and green pepper in butter for about 10 minutes or until tender. Remove from skillet with slotted spoon, leaving butter in skillet. Set vegetables aside.
3. Dry veal on paper towel. Bread on one side only, dipping first in flour, then in beaten egg, and last in bread crumbs mixed with Parmesan cheese.
4. Lay a slice of prosciutto on one half of unbreaded side of veal. Fold other side over. Pan-fry for 6 minutes on one side in butter in skillet, adding more butter if needed. Turn veal, and remove skillet from heat.
5. Insert a slice of cheese, and ¼ of the mushroom-pepper mixture into the fold of each steak.
6. Return to heat and cook 6 minutes, or until meat is tender.

Veal Cutlet in Wine with Olives

ABOUT
6 SERVINGS

1½ pounds veal cutlets, cut about ¼ inch thick
¼ cup all-purpose flour
1 teaspoon salt
¼ teaspoon pepper
2 to 3 tablespoons butter or margarine
⅓ cup marsala
⅓ cup sliced green olives

1. Place meat on flat working surface and pound with meat hammer to increase tenderness. Turn meat and repeat process. Cut into 6 serving-size pieces. Coat with a mixture of flour, salt, and pepper.
2. Heat butter in skillet over low heat. Brown meat over medium heat. Add marsala and green olives. Cover skillet and cook over low heat about 1 hour, or until meat is tender when pierced with a fork.

Veal Peasant Style

6 TO 8
SERVINGS

2 tablespoons butter
1 tablespoon olive oil
1 cup finely chopped onion
⅓ cup finely chopped celery
1½ to 2 pounds veal, cubed
1 teaspoon salt
¼ teaspoon pepper
4 tomatoes, peeled and coarsely chopped
Several basil leaves or ¼ teaspoon dried basil leaves
¾ cup beef broth
2 tablespoons butter
1 pound fresh green peas, shelled, or 1 package (10 ounces) frozen green peas
3 carrots, diced
½ teaspoon salt
¾ cup hot water
1 tablespoon minced parsley

1. Heat 2 tablespoons butter and the olive oil in a Dutch oven or large saucepot. Add onion and celery; sauté 3 or 4 minutes.
2. Add meat and brown on all sides. Season with 1 teaspoon salt and the pepper. Stir in tomatoes and basil. Cover Dutch oven.
3. Cook at 275°F 1¼ hours, or until meat is almost tender. Add broth, a little at a time, during cooking.
4. Heat 2 tablespoons butter in a saucepan. Stir in peas, carrots, ½ teaspoon salt, and water. Cook, covered, until vegetables are tender (about 15 minutes).
5. Skim off fat from the meat. Stir in the cooked vegetables and parsley. Continue cooking in oven until meat is tender.
6. Serve meat surrounded with the vegetables and **small sauteed potatoes** on a heated platter. Pour sauce over all.

Veal Peasant Style

Veal Scaloppine with Mushrooms and Capers

ABOUT
4 SERVINGS

1 pound veal round steak,
   cut about ½ inch thick
½ cup flour
½ teaspoon salt
⅛ teaspoon pepper
¼ cup olive oil
½ clove garlic, minced
¼ pound mushrooms,
   cleaned and sliced
   lengthwise
1 medium onion, thinly
   sliced
1¾ cups sieved canned
   tomatoes
¼ cup capers
1 teaspoon minced parsley
¼ teaspoon oregano

1. Put meat on a flat working surface and pound on both sides with a meat hammer. Cut into 1-inch pieces. Coat evenly with a mixture of flour, ½ teaspoon salt, and ⅛ teaspoon pepper.
2. Heat oil with garlic in a large skillet. Add veal and slowly brown on both sides.
3. Meanwhile, heat butter in a skillet. Add mushrooms and onion; cook until mushrooms are lightly browned.
4. Add mushrooms to veal along with tomatoes, capers, 1 teaspoon salt, ⅛ teaspoon pepper, parsley, and oregano; mix well.
5. Cover skillet and simmer about 25 minutes, or until veal is tender; stir occasionally.

Curried Veal and Vegetables

ABOUT
6 SERVINGS

1 pound veal for stew (1-inch
   cubes)
2 cups water
1 teaspoon salt
3 medium carrots, pared and
   cut in quarters
½ pound green beans
2 large stalks celery, cut in
   ½-inch slices
3 tablespoons butter or
   margarine
2 tablespoons flour
½ teaspoon curry powder
¼ teaspoon salt
Cooked rice
Fresh parsley, snipped

1. Put veal into a large saucepan with water and 1 teaspoon salt. Cover, bring to boiling, reduce heat, and simmer 1 hour. Add carrots, green beans, and celery. Cover, bring to boiling, and simmer 1 hour, or until meat is tender.
2. Remove meat and vegetables from broth with a slotted spoon; set aside. Reserve broth.
3. Heat butter in a saucepan. Blend in flour, curry powder, and ¼ teaspoon salt. Heat until bubbly. Add reserved broth gradually, stirring until smooth. Bring to boiling, stirring constantly, and cook 1 to 2 minutes. Mix in meat and vegetables. Heat thoroughly.
4. Serve over rice. Sprinkle with parsley.

German Veal Chops

4 SERVINGS

4 veal loin or rib chops
Butter or margarine
2 medium onions, sliced
1 cup dark beer
1 bay leaf
½ teaspoon salt
Dash pepper
2 tablespoons flour

1. Brown veal in butter in a skillet; set meat aside. Sauté onion in same skillet until golden.
2. Add beer, bay leaf, salt, and pepper. Cover and simmer 15 minutes.
3. Transfer veal and onion to a platter. Make a paste of flour and a little water; stir into cooking liquid in skillet. Cook, stirring constantly, until thickened and smooth. Pour over veal and onion.

Note: If you do not have dark beer, add **½ teaspoon molasses** to light beer.

Lamb Crown Roast with Mint Stuffing

ABOUT
8 SERVINGS

8 slices enriched white bread, toasted and cubed
1 unpared red apple, cored and diced
1½ tablespoons coarsely chopped mint or 1½ teaspoons dried mint flakes
¾ teaspoon poultry seasoning
½ teaspoon salt
6 tablespoons butter
½ cup chopped celery
¼ cup chopped onion
½ cup water
1 lamb rib crown roast (5 to 6 pounds)

1. Combine toasted bread cubes, apple, mint, poultry seasoning, and salt in a large bowl.
2. Heat butter in a saucepan. Mix in celery and onion and cook about 5 minutes. Pour over bread mixture along with water; toss lightly.
3. Place lamb on a rack, rib ends up, in a shallow roasting pan. Fill center with stuffing.
4. Roast in a 325°F oven about 2½ hours, or until a meat thermometer registers 175° to 180°F (depending on desired degree of doneness).
5. Place roast on a heated serving platter. Prepare gravy, if desired. Accompany with Parsley-Buttered New Potatoes (page 42) and Butter-Sauced Asparagus (page 36).

Lamb Curry

6 SERVINGS

1½ pounds boneless lamb shoulder, cut in ¾-inch cubes
2 tablespoons shortening
1 teaspoon salt
1 teaspoon paprika
¼ teaspoon pepper
1 large onion, sliced
1 cup sliced celery
2¼ cups water
1 teaspoon curry powder
¼ cup flour
1 cup uncooked white rice

1. Brown lamb in shortening in a large saucepan. Sprinkle with salt, paprika, and pepper. Add onion, celery, and 2 cups water. Cover and simmer 1 hour, or until tender.
2. Combine curry powder, flour, and remaining ¼ cup water. Gradually add to saucepan, stirring until thickened and smooth.
3. Meanwhile, prepare rice according to package directions. Press rice in bottom and up sides of a 2-quart casserole. Pour lamb mixture into rice shell.
4. Bake, covered, at 350°F 20 minutes, or until casserole is bubbly. Serve with **chopped peanuts, shredded coconut,** and **chutney**.

Lamb Kabobs

6 SERVINGS

1½ pounds lamb (leg, loin, or shoulder), boneless, cut in 1½-inch cubes
½ cup vegetable oil
1 tablespoon lemon juice
2 teaspoons sugar
½ teaspoon salt
½ teaspoon paprika
¼ teaspoon dry mustard
⅛ teaspoon ground black pepper
¼ teaspoon Worcestershire sauce
1 clove garlic, cut in halves
6 small whole cooked potatoes
6 small whole cooked onions
Butter or margarine, melted
6 plum tomatoes

1. Put lamb cubes into a shallow dish. Combine oil, lemon juice, sugar, salt, paprika, dry mustard, pepper, Worcestershire sauce, and garlic. Pour over meat. Cover and marinate at least 1 hour in refrigerator, turning pieces occasionally. Drain.
2. Alternately thread lamb cubes, potatoes, and onions on 6 skewers. Brush pieces with melted butter.
3. Broil 3 to 4 inches from heat about 15 minutes, or until lamb is desired degree of doneness; turn frequently and brush with melted butter. Shortly before kabobs are done, impale tomatoes on ends of skewers.

Roast Leg of Lamb with Spicy Wine Sauce

12 TO 16 SERVINGS

1 cup dry red wine
¼ cup salad oil
1 onion, coarsely chopped
2 cloves garlic, minced
½ teaspoon Tabasco
2 teaspoons salt
1 lamb leg whole (6 to 8 pounds)
Parsley

1. Combine wine, oil, onion, garlic, Tabasco, and salt; pour over lamb. Cover and refrigerate 6 hours or overnight, turning occasionally.
2. Place lamb on rack in shallow roasting pan. Roast at 325°F about 25 minutes per pound, or until meat thermometer registers 160° to 170°F (medium); baste occasionally with marinade.
3. Garnish with parsley.

Smothered Lamb Chops

6 SERVINGS

6 lamb rib chops
2 tablespoons butter or margarine
4 medium red potatoes, pared and thinly sliced
2 large onions, sliced
1½ cups beef bouillon
2 tablespoons snipped parsley
¼ cup buttered bread crumbs

1. Brown lamb chops on both sides in butter in a skillet. Place in a 2-quart shallow baking dish.
2. Arrange potatoes over chops and onions over potatoes. Season lightly with **salt.** Pour bouillon over all.
3. Bake, covered, at 375°F 1 hour, or until chops and vegetables are tender. Combine parsley and bread crumbs. Remove cover from casserole. Sprinkle with the parsley-bread crumbs. Bake, uncovered at 450°F 10 minutes, or until crumbs are lightly browned.

Pork Loin Roast

8 TO 10 SERVINGS

1 pork loin roast (4 to 6 pounds)
Salt and pepper
Spiced crab apples

1. Have the butcher saw across the rib bones of roast at base of the backbone, separating the ribs from the backbone. Place roast, fat side up, on a rack in an open roasting pan. Season with salt and pepper. Insert meat thermometer in roast so the bulb is centered in the thickest part and not resting on bone or in fat.
2. Roast in a 350°F oven about 2½ to 3 hours, or until thermometer registers 170°F; allow 30 to 40 minutes per pound.
3. For easy carving, remove backbone, place roast on platter, and allow roast to set for 15 to 20 minutes. Garnish platter with spiced crab apples, heated if desired.

Barbecued Spareribs à la Marinade

ABOUT 6 SERVINGS

1 package 15-minute meat marinade
⅔ cup cold water
4 pounds pork spareribs

1. Combine meat marinade and water in a large shallow pan; blend thoroughly.
2. Put ribs into marinade. Pierce all surfaces of meat deeply and thoroughly with fork to carry flavor deep down. Marinate only 15 minutes, turning several times. Remove meat from marinade; reserve for basting.
3. Place ribs on grill 4 to 6 inches from hot coals. Cook

until crispy brown, about 1 hour, turning and brushing with marinade frequently. Use kitchen shears to cut ribs into pieces for serving.

Bavarian Casserole

4 SERVINGS

2 celery stalks, chopped
1 medium onion, chopped
3 tablespoons butter or margarine
½ teaspoon salt
¼ teaspoon sage
¼ teaspoon sugar
⅛ teaspoon pepper
1 cup beer
4 cups pumpernickel bread cubes (5 slices)
2 cups cubed cooked pork (10 ounces)

1. Sauté celery and onion in butter until soft; stir in seasonings. Add beer.
2. Place bread and pork in a 1½-quart casserole. Add beer-vegetable mixture. Stir lightly.
3. Cover and bake at 375°F 30 to 35 minutes.

Neapolitan Pork Chops

6 SERVINGS

2 tablespoons olive oil
1 clove garlic, minced
6 pork rib or loin chops, cut about ¾ to 1 inch thick
1 teaspoon salt
¼ teaspoon pepper
1 pound mushrooms, cleaned and sliced
2 green peppers, cleaned and chopped
½ cup canned tomatoes, sieved
3 tablespoons dry white wine

1. Heat oil in a large, heavy skillet. Add garlic and cook until lightly browned.
2. Season chops with salt and pepper. Put chops in skillet and brown on both sides.
3. Add mushrooms, green pepper, sieved tomato, and wine. Cover and cook over low heat about 1 hour, or until tender.

Northwoods Pork Chop

4 SERVINGS

1 package (2¾ ounces) instant wild rice
¼ cup chopped celery
¼ cup chopped green pepper
¼ cup chopped onion
6 tablespoons butter or margarine
4 pork chops, ¾ inch thick
¼ cup flour
2 cups milk
½ teaspoon salt
⅛ teaspoon pepper
½ cup (2 ounces) shredded American cheese

1. Prepare wild rice according to package directions.
2. Sauté celery, green pepper, and onion in 4 tablespoons butter in a skillet. Combine with wild rice. Put into a 1½-quart shallow baking dish.
3. Brown pork chops on both sides in skillet. Place on top of wild rice mixture.
4. Melt remaining 2 tablespoons butter in skillet. Blend in flour. Gradually add milk, stirring until thickened and smooth. Add salt and pepper. Pour over pork chops.
5. Bake, covered, at 350°F 1 hour, or until chops are done. Sprinkle with cheese.

Chinatown Chop Suey

8 SERVINGS

1¼ pounds pork, boneless
1 pound beef, boneless
¾ pound veal, boneless
3 tablespoons cooking oil
1 cup water
3 cups diagonally sliced celery
2 cups coarsely chopped onion
3 tablespoons cornstarch
¼ cup water
¼ cup soy sauce
¼ cup bead molasses
1 can (16 ounces) bean sprouts, drained and rinsed
2 cans (5 ounces each) water chestnuts, drained and sliced

1. Cut meat into 2x½x¼-inch strips. Heat oil in a large wok. Stir-fry ½ pound of meat at a time, browning pieces on all sides. Remove the meat from the wok as it is browned. When all the meat is browned, return it to the wok. Cover and cook over low heat 30 minutes.
2. Mix in 1 cup water, celery, and onions. Bring to boiling and simmer, covered, 20 minutes.
3. Blend cornstarch, the ¼ cup water, soy sauce, and molasses. Stir into meat mixture. Bring to boiling and cook 2 minutes, stirring constantly. Mix in bean sprouts and water chestnuts; heat.
4. Serve on **hot fluffy rice.**

Lagered Ham and Noodle Casserole

6 SERVINGS

1 medium green pepper, chopped
1 medium onion, chopped
¼ cup butter or margarine
3 tablespoons flour
½ teaspoon dry mustard
½ teaspoon salt
Dash pepper
⅓ cup instant nonfat dry milk
1 can or bottle (12 ounces) beer
1 cup shredded Cheddar cheese (4 ounces)
8 ounces medium noodles, cooked and drained
2 cups diced cooked ham (⅔ pound)

1. For sauce, slowly sauté green pepper and onion in butter until soft and almost tender. Stir in flour and seasonings.
2. Mix dry milk and ⅓ cup beer.
3. Gradually add remaining beer to flour mixture. Cook, stirring constantly, until thickened and bubbly. Add cheese; stir until melted. Remove from heat; add beer-milk mixture.
4. Combine sauce, cooked noodles, and ham. Turn into a 2½-quart casserole.
5. Bake at 350°F 20 minutes, or until heated through and bubbly.

Fruited Pork Roast, Scandinavian Style

8 SERVINGS

1 pork rolled loin roast, boneless (3 to 3½ pounds)
8 to 10 pitted dried prunes
1 can or bottle (12 ounces) beer
½ teaspoon ginger
1 medium apple, pared and chopped
1 teaspoon lemon juice
½ teaspoon salt
Dash pepper
¼ cup flour

1. Make pocket down center of roast by piercing with a long, sharp tool such as a steel knife sharpener; leave string on roast. (Alternate method: Remove string. Using strong knife, cut pocket in pork by making a deep slit down length of loin, going to within ½ inch of the two ends and within 1 inch of other side.)
2. Meanwhile, combine prunes, beer, and ginger in a saucepan; heat to boiling. Remove from heat; let stand 30 minutes.
3. Mix apple with lemon juice to prevent darkening. Drain prunes, reserving liquid; pat dry with paper towels. Mix prunes and apple.
4. Pack fruit into pocket in pork, using handle of wooden spoon to pack tightly. (With alternate method of cutting pocket, tie with sring at 1-inch intervals. Secure with skewers or sew with kitchen thread.)

5. Place meat on rack in a roasting pan.

6. Roast at 350°F 2 to 2½ hour, allowing 40 to 45 minutes per pound. During last 45 minutes of roasting, spoon fat from pan; baste occasionally with liquid drained from prunes.

7. Transfer meat to a platter. Skim fat from cooking liquid; measure liquid. Add a little water to roasting pan to help loosen brown bits; add to cooking liquid. Add salt, pepper, and enough additional water to measure 2 cups total. Make a paste of flour and a little more water. Combine with cooking liquid. Cook, stirring constantly, until thickened. Pass in a sauceboat for pouring over meat slices.

Apple-Covered Ham in Claret

6 TO 8 SERVINGS

2 smoked ham center slices, fully cooked, about ¾ inch thick (about ½ pound each) or 1 large center cut 1½ inches thick
½ teaspoon dry mustard
3 to 4 medium Golden Delicious apples, cored and cut in rings
4 orange slices
¾ cup dry red wine, such as claret
½ cup packed brown sugar
Parsley sprigs

1. Place ham slices in large shallow baking dish. Sprinkle each slice with ¼ teaspoon mustard.

2. Cut unpared apple rings in half and place around outer edge of ham, slightly overlapping slices.

3. Place two orange slices in center of each ham slice.

4. Pour wine over top of ham and fruit. Then sprinkle entire dish with brown sugar.

5. Cover; cook in a 350°F oven 45 minutes. Serve on platter or from baking dish, and garnish with parsley.

Hearty Sausage Supper

4 SERVINGS

1 jar (16 ounces) applesauce
1 can (14 ounces) sauerkraut, drained
⅓ cup dry white wine
2 tablespoons firmly packed brown sugar
1 can (16 ounces) small white potatoes, drained
1 can (16 ounces) small whole onions, drained
1 ring (12 ounces) Polish sausage, slashed several times
1 tablespoon snipped parsley

1. mix applesauce, sauerkraut, wine, and brown sugar. Put into a 2½-quart casserole.

2. Arrange potatoes and onions around edge of casserole. Place sausage in center.

3. Bake, covered, at 350°F 45 to 50 minutes, or until heated through. Sprinkle with parsley.

Smoked Sausage Dinner

4 SERVINGS

1 medium onion, chopped
½ cup chopped green pepper
2 tablespoons butter or margarine
1 pound smoked sausage, cut in ½-inch pieces
1 can (16 ounces) tomatoes, cut up
1 cup uncooked noodles

1. Sauté onion and green pepper in butter in a skillet. Add sausage and brown lightly; drain off excess fat.

2. Stir in remaining ingredients. Put into a 1½-quart casserole.

3. Bake, covered, at 375°F 45 minutes, or until noodles are tender, stirring once.

Poultry

Chicken and Dumplings

ABOUT
8 SERVINGS

¼ cup butter or margarine
2 broiler-fryer chickens, cut
in serving-size pieces
½ cup chopped onion
¼ cup chopped celery
2 tablespoons chopped celery
leaves
1 clove garlic, minced
¼ cup enriched all-purpose
flour
4 cups chicken broth
1 teaspoon sugar
2 teaspoons salt
¼ teaspoon ground black
pepper
1 teaspoon basil leaves
2 bay leaves
¼ cup chopped parsley
Basil Dumplings
2 packages (10 ounces each)
frozen green peas

1. Heat butter in a large skillet. Add chicken pieces and brown on all sides. Remove chicken from skillet.
2. Add onion, celery, celery leaves, and garlic to fat in skillet. Cook until vegetables are tender. Sprinkle with flour and mix well. Add chicken broth, sugar, salt, pepper, basil, bay leaves, and parsley; bring to boiling, stirring constantly. Return chicken to skillet and spoon sauce over it; cover.
3. Cook in a 350°F oven 40 minutes.
4. Shortly before cooking time is completed, prepare Basil Dumplings.
5. Remove skillet from oven and turn control to 425°F. Stir peas into skillet mixture and bring to boiling. Drop dumpling dough onto stew.
6. Return to oven and cook, uncovered, 10 minutes; cover and cook 10 minutes, or until chicken is tender and dumplings are done.

Basil Dumplings: Combine **2 cups all-purpose biscuit mix** and **1 teaspoon basil leaves** in a bowl. Add **⅔ cup milk** and stir with a fork until a dough is formed. Proceed as directed in recipe.

Country Captain

ABOUT
6 SERVINGS

1 broiler-fryer chicken (3 to
3½ pounds), cut in serving-
size pieces
¼ cup enriched all-purpose
flour
½ teaspoon salt
Pinch ground white pepper
3 to 4 tablespoons lard
2 onions, finely chopped
2 medium green peppers,
chopped
1 clove garlic, crushed in a
garlic press or minced
1½ teaspoons salt
½ teaspoon ground white
pepper
1½ teaspoons curry powder
½ teaspoon ground thyme
½ teaspoon snipped parsley
5 cups undrained canned
tomatoes
2 cups hot cooked rice
¼ cup dried currants
¾ cup roasted blanched
almonds
Parsley sprigs

1. Remove skin from chicken. Mix flour, ½ teaspoon salt, and pinch white pepper. Coat chicken pieces.
2. Melt lard in a large heavy skillet; add chicken and brown on all sides. Remove pieces from skillet and keep hot.
3. Cook onions, peppers, and garlic in the same skillet, stirring occasionally until onion is lightly browned. Blend 1½ teaspoons salt, ½ teaspoon white pepper, curry powder, and thyme. Mix into skillet along with parsley and tomatoes.
4. Arrange chicken in a shallow roasting pan and pour tomato mixture over it. (If it does not cover chicken, add a small amount of water to the skillet in which mixture was cooked and pour liquid over chicken.) Place a cover on pan or cover tightly with aluminum foil.
5. Cook in a 350°F oven about 45 minutes, or until chicken is tender.
6. Arrange chicken in center of a large heated platter and pile the hot rice around it. Stir currants into sauce remaining in the pan and pour over the rice. Scatter almonds over top. Garnish with parsley.

Skillet Chicken and Vegetables

6 SERVINGS

1 can (about 10 ounces) condensed chicken broth
1 cup dry white wine, such as chablis
1 tablespoon instant minced onion
½ teaspoon salt
1 bay leaf
¼ teaspoon rosemary, crushed
6 half breasts of chicken
6 small carrots
6 small zucchini
2 tablespoons cornstarch
2 tablespoons cold water
3 tablespoons chopped pimento
2 tablespoons chopped parsley

1. Combine broth, wine, onion, salt, bay leaf, and rosemary in a large skillet. Heat to boiling.
2. Place chicken breasts in the boiling liquid; cover and simmer 20 minutes.
3. While chicken is cooking, pare carrots and cut in half lengthwise. Cut zucchini in half lengthwise. Add carrots and zucchini to the chicken; cover, and cook 15 minutes longer, or until chicken is tender and vegetables are crisp-tender.
4. Remove chicken and vegetables with a slotted spoon; keep warm.
5. Mix cornstarch with water and stir into liquid remaining in skillet. Cook, stirring until sauce boils thoroughly. Add pimento and parsley, and pour over chicken and vegetables. Serve immediately.

Crunchy Fried Chicken

4 SERVINGS

1 cup all-purpose flour
½ teaspoon salt
¼ teaspoon pepper
2 eggs
½ cup beer
1 broiler-fryer chicken (2 to 2½ pounds), cut up
Cooking oil

1. Mix flour, salt, and pepper. Beat eggs with beer; add to flour mixture. Stir until smooth.
2. Dip chicken in batter, coating pieces well. Chill 1 hour.
3. Fry chicken in hot oil ½ to 1 inch deep 15 minutes on one side. Turn; fry on other side 5 to 10 minutes, or until browned and done. Drain on absorbent paper.

Chicken Polynesian Style

ABOUT
6 SERVINGS

2 cups chicken broth
1 package (10 ounces) frozen mixed vegetables
½ cup diagonally sliced celery
1½ tablespoons cornstarch
½ teaspoon sugar
½ teaspoon seasoned salt
⅛ teaspoon ground black pepper
½ teaspoon Worcestershire sauce
1 small clove garlic, minced or crushed in a garlic press
1 tablespoon instant minced onion
1 can (6 ounces) ripe olives, drained and cut in wedges
Cooked chicken, cut in 1-inch pieces (about 2 cups)
Chow mein noodles
Salted peanuts
Soy sauce

1. Heat ½ cup chicken broth in a saucepan. Add frozen vegetables and celery; cook, covered, until crisp-tender. Remove vegetables and set aside; reserve any cooking liquid in saucepan.
2. Mix cornstarch, sugar, seasoned salt, and pepper; blend with ¼ cup of the chicken broth. Add remaining broth, Worcestershire sauce, garlic, and onion to the saucepan. Add cornstarch mixture; bring to boiling, stirring constantly. Cook and stir 2 to 3 minutes.
3. Mix in olives, chicken, and reserved vegetables; heat thoroughly, stirring occasionally.
4. Serve over chow mein noodles and top generously with peanuts. Accompany with a cruet of soy sauce.

Chicken with Fruit

ABOUT
6 SERVINGS

1 tablespoon flour
1 teaspoon seasoned salt
¾ teaspoon paprika
3 pounds broiler-fryer
  chicken pieces (legs, thighs,
  and breasts)
1½ tablespoons vegetable oil
1½ tablespoons butter or
  margarine
1 clove garlic, crushed in a
  garlic press or minced
⅓ cup chicken broth
2 tablespoons cider vinegar
1 tablespoon brown sugar
¼ teaspoon rosemary
1 can (11 ounces) mandarin
  oranges, drained; reserve
  syrup
1 jar (4 ounces) maraschino
  cherries, drained; reserve
  syrup
1 tablespoon water
1 tablespoon cornstarch
½ cup dark seedless raisins
Cooked rice

1. Mix flour, seasoned salt, and paprika. Coat chicken pieces.
2. Heat oil, butter, and garlic in a large heavy skillet. Add chicken pieces and brown well on all sides.
3. Mix broth, vinegar, brown sugar, rosemary, and reserved syrups. Pour into skillet; cover and cook slowly 25 minutes, or until chicken is tender.
4. Remove chicken pieces to a serving dish and keep warm; skim any excess fat from liquid in skillet. Blend water with cornstarch and stir into liquid in skillet. Add raisins, bring to boiling, stirring constantly, and cook about 5 minutes, or until mixture is thickened and smooth. Mix in orange sections and cherries; heat thoroughly.
5. Pour sauce over chicken and serve with hot fluffy rice.

Chicken Fricassee with Vegetables

ABOUT
4 SERVINGS

1 broiler-fryer chicken
  (about 3 pounds), cut in
  serving-size pieces
1½ teaspoons salt
1 bay leaf
Water
2 cups sliced carrots
2 onions, quartered
2 crookneck squashes, cut in
  halves lengthwise
2 pattypan squashes, cut in
  halves
Green beans (about 6
  ounces), tips cut off
1 can (3½ ounces) pitted
  ripe olives, drained
1 tablespoon cornstarch
2 tablespoons water

1. Place chicken pieces along with salt and bay leaf in a Dutch oven or saucepot. Add enough water to just cover chicken. Bring to boiling; simmer, covered, 25 minutes until chicken is almost tender.
2. Add carrots and onions to cooking liquid; cook, covered, 10 minutes. Add squashes and green beans to cooking liquid; cook, covered, 10 minutes, or until chicken and vegetables are tender. Remove chicken and vegetables to a warm serving dish and add olives; keep hot.
3. Blend cornstarch and 2 tablespoons water; stir into boiling cooking liquid. Boil 2 to 3 minutes. Pour gravy over chicken.

Country-Flavored Chicken Halves

4 SERVINGS

1 package 15-minute chicken
  marinade
1 cup cold water
1 broiler-fryer (2½ to 3
  pounds), cut in half

1. In a shallow pan, thoroughly blend chicken marinade and water. Place well-drained chicken in marinade; turn, pierce all surfaces of chicken deeply with fork. Marinade only 15 minutes, turning several times. Remove chicken from marinade and arrange skin side up in a shallow ungreased pan just large enough to accommodate the chicken.
2. Bake uncovered, at 425°F for 45 to 55 minutes, until thoroughly cooked.

Chicken Mexicana

ABOUT
6 SERVINGS

3 tablespoons vegetable oil
2 broiler-fryer chickens (2½ to 3 pounds each), cut in serving-size pieces
2 cans (8 ounces each) tomato sauce
1 can (13¾ ounces) chicken broth
2 tablespoons (½ envelope) dry onion soup mix
¾ cup chopped onion
1 clove garlic, minced
6 tablespoons crunchy peanut butter
½ cup cream
½ teaspoon chili powder
¼ cup dry sherry
Cooked rice

1. Heat oil in a large skillet. Add chicken and brown on all sides.
2. Meanwhile, combine tomato sauce, 1 cup chicken broth, soup mix, onion, and garlic in a saucepan. Heat thoroughly, stirring constantly.
3. Pour sauce over chicken in skillet. Simmer, covered, 20 minutes.
4. Put peanut butter into a bowl and blend in cream and remaining chicken broth; stir into skillet along with chili powder and sherry. Heat thoroughly. Serve with hot fluffy rice.

Chicken Cacciatore

ABOUT
6 SERVINGS

¼ cup cooking oil
1 broiler-fryer (2½ pounds), cut up
2 onions, sliced
2 cloves garlic, minced
3 tomatoes, cored and quartered
2 green peppers, sliced
1 small bay leaf
1 teaspoon salt
¼ teaspoon pepper
½ teaspoon celery seed
1 teaspoon crushed oregano or basil
1 can (8 ounces) tomato sauce
¼ cup sauterne
8 ounces spaghetti, cooked according to package directions

1. Heat oil in a large, heavy skillet; add chicken and brown on all sides. Remove from skillet.
2. Add onion and garlic to oil remaining in skillet and cook until onion is tender, but not brown; stir occasionally.
3. Return chicken to skillet and add the tomatoes, green pepper, and bay leaf.
4. Mix salt, pepper, celery seed, and oregano and blend with tomato sauce; pour over all.
5. Cover and cook over low heat 45 minutes. Blend in wine and cook, uncovered, 20 minutes longer. Discard bay leaf.
6. Put the cooked spaghetti onto a hot serving platter and top with the chicken and sauce.

Chicken and Tomato Casserole

4 SERVINGS

1 broiler-fryer chicken (about 3 pounds), cut up
3 tablespoons shortening
½ cup chopped onion
¼ cup chopped green pepper
1 can (28 ounces) tomatoes (undrained)
1 can (8 ounces) tomato sauce
1 can (6 ounces) tomato paste
1 teaspoon salt
1 teaspoon oregano

1. Brown chicken in shortening in a skillet. Place in a 2-quart casserole.
2. Sauté onion and green pepper in fat in skillet. Stir in remaining ingredients and pour over chicken.
3. Bake, covered, at 350°F 1 hour, or until chicken is tender. Serve with **hot, cooked spaghetti.**

Herb-Chicken with Mushrooms

ABOUT
4 SERVINGS

2 tablespoons butter or
margarine
1 broiler-fryer chicken (3
pounds), cut in quarters
¾ cup cider vinegar
¼ cup water
1 cup (about 3 ounces) sliced
mushrooms
1 tablespoon finely chopped
parsley
1 tablespoon finely chopped
chives
1 teaspoon crushed tarragon
½ teaspoon thyme
½ teaspoon salt
¼ teaspoon black pepper
2 tablespoons flour
1½ cups chicken broth
½ cup sherry

1. Heat butter in a large skillet. Place chicken pieces, skin side down, in skillet and brown on all sides.
2. Meanwhile, pour a mixture of vinegar and water over the mushrooms. Let stand 10 minutes; drain.
3. When chicken is evenly browned, transfer pieces to a shallow baking dish. Sprinkle the seasonings over the chicken. Spoon drained mushrooms over the top; sprinkle evenly with flour. Pour broth and wine over all.
4. Bake at 325°F about 1 hour, or until tender.

Roast Turkey with Herbed Stuffing

ABOUT
25 SERVINGS

Cooked Giblets and Broth
4 quarts ½-inch enriched
bread cubes
1 cup snipped parsley
2 to 2½ teaspoons salt
2 teaspoons thyme
2 teaspoons rosemary,
crushed
2 teaspoons marjoram
1 teaspoon ground sage
1 cup butter or margarine
1 cup coarsely chopped
onion
1 cup coarsely chopped
celery with leaves
1 turkey (14 to 15 pounds)
Fat
3 tablespoons flour
¼ teaspoon salt
⅛ teaspoon ground black
pepper

1. Prepare Cooked Giblets and Broth. Measure 1 cup chopped cooked giblets; set the broth aside.
2. Combine bread cubes, reserved giblets, and parsley in a large bowl. Blend salt, thyme, rosemary, marjoram, and sage; add to bread mixture and toss to mix.
3. Heat butter in a skillet. Mix in onion and celery; cook about 5 minutes, stirring occasionally. Toss with the bread mixture.
4. Add 1 to 2 cups broth (depending upon how moist a stuffing is desired), mixing lightly until ingredients are thoroughly blended.
5. Rinse turkey with cold water; pat dry, inside and out, with absorbent paper. Lightly fill body and neck cavities with the stuffing. Fasten neck skin to back with a skewer. Bring wing tips onto back of bird. Push drumsticks under band of skin at tail, if present, or tie to tail with cord.
6. Place turkey, breast side up, on rack in a shallow roasting pan. Brush skin with fat. Insert meat thermometer in the thickest part of the inner thigh muscle, being sure that tip does not touch bone.
7. Roast in a 325°F oven about 5 hours, or until thermometer registers 180°F to 185°F. If desired, baste or brush bird occasionally with pan drippings. Place turkey on a heated platter; for easier carving, allow turkey to stand about 30 minutes.
8. Meanwhile, leaving brown residue in roasting pan, pour remaining drippings and fat into a bowl. Allow fat to rise to surface; skim off fat and measure 3 tablespoons into roasting pan. Blend flour, salt, and pepper with fat. Cook and stir until bubbly. Continue to stir while slowly adding

2 cups reserved liquid (broth and drippings). Cook, stirring constantly, until gravy thickens; scrape pan to blend in brown residue. Cook 1 to 2 minutes. If desired, mix in finely chopped cooked giblets the last few minutes of cooking.

Cooked Giblets and Broth: Put **turkey neck** and **giblets** (except liver) into a saucepan with **1 large onion,** sliced, **parsley, celery with leaves, 1 medium bay leaf, 2 teaspoons salt,** and **1 cup water.** Cover, bring to boiling, reduce heat, and simmer until giblets are tender (about 2 hours); add the liver the last 15 minutes of cooking. Strain through a colander or sieve; reserve broth for stuffing. Chop giblets; set aside for stuffing and gravy.

Turkey-Oyster Casserole

ABOUT
6 SERVINGS

1 tablespoon butter
2 teaspoons grated onion
4 ounces mushrooms, sliced
    lengthwise
¼ cup butter
¼ cup enriched all-purpose
    flour
1 teaspoon salt
¼ teaspoon ground pepper
Few grains cayenne pepper
2 cups milk
1 egg yolk, slightly beaten
2 tablespoons chopped
    parsley
¼ teaspoon thyme
2 drops Tabasco
1 pint oysters (with liquor)
2 cups diced cooked turkey
Buttered soft enriched bread
    crumbs

1. Heat 1 tablespoon butter with onion in a skillet; add mushrooms and cook over medium heat until slightly browned, stirring occasionally. Set aside.
2. Heat ¼ cup butter in a saucepan over low heat. Stir in flour, salt, pepper, and cayenne; cook until bubbly. Add milk gradually, stirring until well blended. Bring rapidly to boiling and boil 1 to 2 minutes, stirring constantly.
3. Blend a small amount of the hot sauce into egg yolk and return to remaining sauce, stirring until mixed. Stir in parsley, thyme, and Tabasco.
4. Heat oysters just to boiling; drain. Add oysters, turkey, and the mushrooms to sauce; toss lightly until thoroughly mixed.
5. Turn mixture into a buttered shallow 1½-quart baking dish. Sprinkle with crumbs.
6. Heat in a 400°F oven about 10 minutes, or until mixture is bubbly around edges and crumbs are golden brown.

Duck with Red Cabbage

ABOUT
4 SERVINGS

1 head red cabbage,
    shredded
1 onion, chopped
Salt
6 ounces salt pork, diced
½ cup red wine or chicken
    broth
1 duck (5 to 6 pounds)

1. Put cabbage and onion in a bowl, sprinkle with salt, and let stand 10 minutes. Squeeze out liquid.
2. Fry salt pork in a skillet until golden. Add cabbage-onion mixture and wine. Cover and simmer 20 minutes.
3. Place duck in a roasting pan.
4. Bake at 425°F 30 minutes. Drain off fat. Spoon cabbage mixture over duck. Reduce oven temperature to 350°F. Bake about 45 minutes, or until duck is tender. Baste frequently.

Glazed Duckling Gourmet

6 TO 8
SERVINGS

2 ducklings (about 4 pounds each), quartered (do not use wings, necks, and backs) and skinned
1½ teaspoons salt
¼ teaspoon ground nutmeg
3 to 4 tablespoons butter
1 clove garlic, minced
1½ teaspoons rosemary, crushed
1½ teaspoons thyme
1½ cups burgundy
2 teaspoons red wine vinegar
⅓ cup currant jelly
2 teaspoons cornstarch
2 tablespoons cold water
1½ cups halved seedless green grapes
Watercress

1. Remove excess fat from duckling pieces; rinse duckling and pat dry with absorbent paper. Rub pieces with salt and nutmeg.
2. Heat butter and garlic in a large skillet over medium heat; add the duckling pieces and brown well on all sides.
3. Add rosemary, thyme, burgundy, vinegar, and jelly to skillet. Bring to boiling; cover and simmer over low heat until duckling is tender (about 45 minutes). Remove duckling to a heated platter and keep it warm.
4. Combine cornstarch and water; blend into liquid in skillet; bring to boiling and cook 1 to 2 minutes, stirring constantly. Add grapes and toss them lightly until thoroughly heated.
5. Pour the hot sauce over duckling; garnish platter with watercress.

Roast Goose with Rice-and-Pickle Stuffing

6 TO 8
SERVINGS

3 cups cooked rice; or 1 package (6 ounces) seasoned white and wild rice mix, cooked following package directions
1 package (7 ounces) herb-seasoned stuffing croutons
2 medium navel oranges, pared and sectioned
2 onions, chopped
1 cup cranberries, rinsed, sorted, and chopped
1 cup sweet mixed pickles, drained and chopped
¼ cup sweet pickle liquid
½ to ¾ cup butter or margarine, melted
2 tablespoons brown sugar
1 goose (8 to 10 pounds)
1 tablespoon salt
¼ teaspoon ground black pepper
2 tablespoons light corn syrup
1½ cups orange juice
½ cup orange marmalade

1. Combine rice, stuffing croutons, orange sections, onions, cranberries, pickles and liquid, butter, and brown sugar in a large bowl; toss lightly until blended.
2. Rinse goose and remove any large layers of fat from the body cavity. Pat dry with absorbent paper. Rub body and neck cavities with salt and pepper.
3. Lightly spoon stuffing into the neck and body cavities. Overlap neck cavity with the skin and skewer to back of goose. Close body cavity with skewers and lace with cord. Loop cord around legs; tighten slightly and tie to a skewer inserted in the back above tail. Rub skin of goose with a little salt, if desired.
4. Put remaining stuffing into a greased casserole and cover; or cook in heavy-duty aluminum foil. Set in oven with goose during final hour of roasting.
5. Place goose, breast side down, on a rack in a large shallow roasting pan.
6. Roast in a 325°F oven 2 hours, removing fat from pan several times during this period.
7. Turn goose, breast side up. Blend corn syrup and 1 cup orange juice. Brush generously over goose. Roast about 1½ hours, or until goose tests done. To test for doneness, move leg gently by grasping end of bone; when done, drumstick-thigh joint moves easily or twists out. Brush frequently during final roasting period with the orange-syrup blend.
8. Transfer goose to a heated serving platter. Spoon 2 tablespoons drippings, the remaining ½ cup orange juice, and marmalade into a small saucepan. Heat thoroughly, stirring to blend. Pour into a serving dish or gravy boat to accompany goose.

Roast Rock Cornish Hen with Wild Rice and Mushrooms

4 TO 8
SERVINGS

1½ cups water
½ teaspoon salt
½ cup wild rice
2 tablespoons butter or
margarine
½ pound mushrooms, sliced
lengthwise through caps
and stems
1 tablespoon finely chopped
onion
3 tablespoons melted butter
or margarine
2 tablespoons madeira
4 Rock Cornish hens, about
1 pound each
2 teaspoons salt
¼ cup unsalted butter, melted
Watercress (optional)

1. Bring the water and salt to boiling in a deep saucepan.
2. Wash rice in a sieve. Add rice gradually to water so that boiling will not stop. Boil rapidly, covered, 30 to 40 minutes, or until a kernel of rice is entirely tender when pressed between fingers. Drain rice in a colander or sieve.
3. While rice is cooking, heat 2 tablespoons butter or margarine in a skillet. Add the mushrooms and onion; cook, stirring occasionally, until mushrooms are lightly browned. Conbine mushrooms, wild rice, melted butter, and madeira; toss gently until mushrooms and butter are evenly distributed throughout rice.
4. Rinse and pat hens with absorbent paper. Rub cavities of the hens with the salt. Lightly fill body cavities with the wild rice stuffing. To close body cavities, sew or skewer and lace with cord. Fasten neck skin to backs and wings to bodies with skewers.
5. Place hens, breast-side up, on rack in roasting pan. Brush each hen with melted unsalted butter (about 1 tablespoon).
6. Roast, uncovered, in a 350°F oven; frequently baste hens during roasting period with drippings from roasting pan. Roast 1 to 1½ hours, or until hens test done. To test, move leg gently by grasping end bone; drumstick-thigh joint moves easily when hens are done. Remove skewers, if used.
7. Transfer hens to a heated serving platter and garnish with sprigs of watercress if desired.

Rock Cornish Hens with Fruited Stuffing

4 SERVINGS

1½ cups herb-seasoned stuffing croutons
½ cup drained canned
apricot halves, cut in pieces
½ cup quartered seedless
green grapes
⅓ cup chopped pecans
¼ cup butter or margarine,
melted
2 tablespoons apricot nectar
1 tablespoon chopped parsley
¼ teaspoon salt
4 Rock Cornish hens (1 to
1½ pounds each), thawed if
purchased frozen
Salt and pepper
⅓ cup apricot nectar
2 teaspoons soy sauce

1. Combine stuffing croutons, apricots, grapes, pecans, 2 tablespoons butter, 2 tablespoons apricot nectar, parsley, and ¼ teaspoon salt in a bowl; mix lightly.
2. Sprinkle cavities of hens with salt and pepper. Fill each hen with about ½ cup stuffing; fasten with skewers and lace with cord.
3. Blend ⅓ cup apricot nectar, soy sauce, and remaining butter. Place hens, breast side up, on a rack in a shallow roasting pan; brush generously with sauce.
4. Roast in a 350°F oven about 1½ hours, or until hens are tender and well browned; baste occasionally with sauce during roasting.

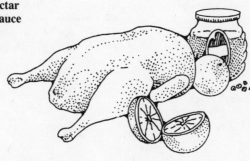

Fish and Shellfish

Broiled Trout

Trout (8- to 10-ounce fish
for each serving)
French dressing
Instant minced onion
Salt
Lemon slices
Tomato wedges
Mint sprigs or watercress

1. Remove head and fins from trout, if desired. Rinse trout quickly under cold running water; dry thoroughly. Brush inside of fish with French dressing and sprinkle generously with instant minced onion and salt. Brush outside generously with French dressing.
2. Arrange trout in a greased shallow baking pan or on a broiler rack. Place under broiler with top of fish about 3 inches from heat. Broil 5 to 8 minutes on each side, or until fish flakes easily; brush with dressing during broiling.
3. Remove trout to heated serving platter and garnish with lemon, tomato, and mint.

Trout Amandine with Pineapple

6 SERVINGS

6 whole trout
Lemon juice
Enriched all-purpose flour
6 tablespoons butter or
margarine
Salt and pepper
2 tablespoons butter or
margarine
½ cup slivered blanched
almonds
6 well-drained canned
pineapple slices
Paprika
Lemon wedges

1. Rinse trout quickly under running cold water; dry thoroughly. Brush trout inside and out with lemon juice. Coat with flour.
2. Heat 6 tablespoons butter in a large skillet. Add trout and brown on both sides. Season with salt and pepper.
3. Meanwhile, heat 2 tablespoons butter in another skillet over low heat. Add almonds and stir occasionally until golden.
4. Sprinkle pineapple slices with paprika. Place pineapple in skillet with almonds and brown lightly on both sides. Arrange trout on a warm serving platter and top with pineapple slices and almonds. Garnish platter with lemon wedges.

Sole with Tangerine Sauce

ABOUT
4 SERVINGS

1 pound sole fillets
5 tablespoons butter or
margarine
2 teaspoons finely shredded
tangerine peel
½ cup tangerine juice
1 teaspoon lemon juice
1 tablespoon finely chopped
parsley
1 tablespoon finely chopped
green onion
1 bay leaf
1 tangerine, peeled, sectioned,
and seeds removed
3 tablespoons flour
½ teaspoon salt
⅛ teaspoon ground black
pepper
3 tablespoons butter or
margarine
Parsley

1. Thaw fish if frozen.
2. Combine 5 tablespoons butter, tangerine peel and juice, lemon juice, 1 tablespoon parsley, green onion, and bay leaf in a saucepan. Bring to boiling and simmer over low heat until slightly thickened, stirring occasionally. Remove from heat; remove bay leaf and mix in tangerine sections. Keep sauce hot.
3. Mix flour, salt, and pepper; coat fish fillets. Heat 3 tablespoons butter in a skillet. Add fillets and fry until both sides are browned and fish flakes easily when tested with a fork.
4. Arrange fish on a hot platter and pour the hot sauce over it. Garnish with parsley.

Planked Fish Fillet Dinner

Fillet of Sole in White Wine

6 SERVINGS

2 pounds sole fillets
½ cup dry white wine
½ cup chopped onion
3 tablespoons butter, melted
2 bay leaves, crushed
1 teaspoon chopped parsley
½ teaspoon salt
¼ teaspoon pepper

1. Put fillets into a greased shallow 2-quart casserole.
2. Mix wine, onion, butter, and dry seasonings. Pour over fish. Cover casserole.
3. Bake at 375°F 25 minutes, or until fish flakes easily when tested with a fork.

Planked Halibut Dinner

4 SERVINGS

4 halibut steaks, fresh or thawed frozen (about 2 pounds)
¼ cup butter, melted
2 tablespoons olive oil
1 tablespoon wine vinegar
2 teaspoons lemon juice
1 clove garlic, minced
¼ teaspoon dry mustard
¼ teaspoon marjoram
½ teaspoon salt
⅛ teaspoon ground black pepper
2 large zucchini
1 package (10 ounces) frozen green peas
1 can (8¼ ounces) tiny whole carrots
Au Gratin Potato Puffs
Butter
Fresh parsley
Lemon wedges

1. Place halibut steaks in an oiled baking pan.
2. Combine butter, olive oil, vinegar, lemon juice, garlic, dry mustard, marjoram, salt, and pepper. Drizzle over halibut.
3. Bake at 450°F 10 to 12 minutes, or until halibut is almost done.
4. Meanwhile, halve zucchini lengthwise and scoop out center portion. Cook in boiling salted water until just tender.
5. Cook peas following directions on package. Heat carrots.
6. Prepare Au Gratin Potato Puffs.
7. Arrange halibut on wooden plank or heated ovenware platter and border with zucchini halves filled with peas, carrots, and potato puffs. Dot peas and carrots with butter.
8. Place platter under broiler to brown potato puffs. Sprinkle carrots with chopped parsley.
9. Garnish with sprigs of parsley and lemon wedges arranged on a skewer.

Au Gratin Potato Puffs: Pare **1½ pounds potatoes**; cook and mash potatoes in a saucepan. Add **2 tablespoons butter** and ⅓ **cup milk**; whip until fluffy. Add **2 slightly beaten egg yolks**, ½ cup shredded sharp Cheddar cheese, **1 teaspoon salt**, and **few grains pepper**; continue whipping. Using a pastry bag with a large star tip, form mounds about 2 inches in diameter on plank. Proceed as directed in recipe.

California Style Red Snapper Steaks

6 SERVINGS

6 fresh or thawed frozen red snapper steaks (about 2 pounds)
Salt and pepper
¼ cup butter or margarine, melted
1 tablespoon grated orange peel
¼ cup orange juice
1 teaspoon lemon juice
Dash nutmeg
Fresh orange sections

1. Arrange red snapper steaks in a single layer in a well-greased baking pan; season with salt and pepper.
2. Combine butter, orange peel and juice, lemon juice, and nutmeg; pour over fish.
3. Bake at 350°F 20 to 25 minutes, or until fish flakes easily when tested with a fork.
4. To serve, put steaks onto a warm platter; spoon sauce in pan over them. Garnish with orange sections.

Blueberry Orange Cheese Cake

Cod Sailor Style

4 SERVINGS

2 pounds cod steaks, about 1 inch thick
2 cups canned tomatoes, sieved
¼ cup chopped green olives
2 tablespoons capers
1 tablespoon parsley
1 teaspoon salt
½ teaspoon pepper
½ teaspoon oregano

1. Put cod steaks into a greased 1½-quart casserole.
2. Combine tomatoes, olives, capers, parsley, salt, pepper, and oregano in a saucepan. Bring to boiling and pour over cod.
3. Bake at 350°F 25 to 30 minutes, or until fish flakes easily when tested with a fork.

Two-Layer Salmon-Rice Loaf

ABOUT 8 SERVINGS

Salmon layer:
1 can (16 ounces) salmon
2 cups coarse soft enriched bread crumbs
2 tablespoons finely chopped onion
½ cup undiluted evaporated milk
1 egg, slightly beaten
2 tablespoons butter or margarine, melted
1 tablespoon lemon juice
1 teaspoon salt

Rice layer:
3 cups cooked enriched rice
¼ cup finely chopped parsley
2 eggs, slightly beaten
⅔ cup undiluted evaporated milk
2 tablespoons butter or margarine, melted
¼ teaspoon salt

Sauce:
1 large onion, quartered and thinly sliced
¾ cup water
1 can (10¾ ounces) condensed tomato soup

1. For salmon layer, drain salmon and remove skin. Flake salmon and put into a bowl. Add bread crumbs, onion, evaporated milk, egg, butter, lemon juice, and salt; mix lightly. Turn into a buttered 9x5x3-inch loaf pan; press lightly to form a layer.
2. For rice layer, combine rice with parsley, eggs, evaporated milk, butter, and salt. Spoon over salmon layer; press lightly.
3. Set filled loaf pan in a shallow pan. Pour hot water into pan to a depth of 1 inch.
4. Bake at 375°F about 45 minutes. Remove from water immediately.
5. Meanwhile, for sauce, put onion and water into a saucepan. Bring to boiling, reduce heat, and simmer, covered, 10 minutes. Remove onion, if desired. Add condensed soup to saucepan, stir until blended, and bring to boiling.
6. Cut loaf into slices and top servings with tomato sauce.

Broiled Salmon

6 SERVINGS

6 salmon steaks, cut ½ inch thick
1 cup sauterne
½ cup vegetable oil
2 tablespoons wine vinegar
2 teaspoons soy sauce
2 tablespoons chopped green onion
Seasoned salt
Green onion, chopped (optional)
Pimento strips (optional)

1. Put salmon steaks into a large shallow dish. Mix sauterne, oil, wine vinegar, soy sauce, and green onion; pour over salmon. Marinate in refrigerator several hours or overnight, turning occasionally.
2. To broil, remove steaks from marinade and place on broiler rack. Set under broiler with top 6 inches from heat. Broil about 5 minutes on each side, brushing generously with marinade several times. About 2 minutes before removing from broiler, sprinkle each steak lightly with seasoned salt and, if desired, top with green onion and pimento. Serve at once.

Planked Fish Fillet Dinner

2 SERVINGS

1 large fish fillet, weighing about 10 ounces (such as sole, flounder, whitefish, lake trout, or haddock)
1 tablespoon melted butter or margarine
Salt and pepper
Seasoned instant potatoes
2 broiled tomato halves
4 broiled mushroom caps (optional)
Lemon slices
Watercress or parsley

1. If fish is frozen, let thaw on refrigerator shelf or at room temperature. Brush seasoned plank lightly with melted butter.
2. Place fish fillet on plank and brush with remaining butter. Sprinkle lightly with salt and pepper. Bake at 350°F for 20 minutes, or just until fish flakes easily.
3. Remove from oven, and turn oven temperature up to 450°F. Pipe a border of hot mashed potatoes along sides of fish.
4. Return to oven for 10 minutes until potatoes are delicately browned. Place tomato halves and mushroom caps, if desired, on plank. Garnish with lemon slices and watercress. Serve at once.

Tuna Fiesta

ABOUT 6 SERVINGS

1 can (6½ to 7 ounces) tuna, drained and separated in large pieces
1 can (16 ounces) stewed tomatoes, drained
1 can (15¼ ounces) spaghetti in tomato sauce with cheese
1 tablespoon ketchup
1 teaspoon seasoned salt
½ cup (about 2 ounces) shredded sharp Cheddar cheese
Few grains paprika
Fresh parsley

1. Turn tuna, stewed tomatoes, and spaghetti into a saucepan. Add ketchup, seasoned salt, cheese, and paprika; mix well. Set over medium heat, stirring occasionally, until thoroughly heated (about 8 minutes).
2. Turn into a warm serving dish; garnish with parsley. Serve at once.

Note: If desired, reserve cheese and paprika for topping. Mix remaining ingredients and turn into a greased 1-quart casserole. Top with the cheese and paprika. Set in a 350°F oven 20 minutes, or until thoroughly heated. Garnish with parsley.

Baked Fish with Shrimp Stuffing

4 TO 6 SERVINGS

1 dressed whitefish, bass, or lake trout (2 to 3 pounds)
Salt
1 cup chopped cooked shrimp
1 cup chopped fresh mushrooms
1 cup soft enriched bread crumbs
½ cup chopped celery
¼ cup chopped onion
2 tablespoons chopped parsley
¾ teaspoon salt
Few grains black pepper
½ teaspoon thyme
¼ cup butter or margarine, melted
2 to 3 tablespoons apple cider
2 tablespoons butter or margarine, melted
Parsley sprigs

1. Rinse fish under running cold water; drain well and pat dry with absorbent paper. Sprinkle fish cavity generously with salt.
2. Combine in a bowl the shrimp, mushrooms, bread crumbs, celery, onion, parsley, salt, pepper, and thyme. Pour ¼ cup melted butter gradually over bread mixture, tossing lightly until mixed.
3. Pile stuffing lightly into fish. Fasten with skewers and lace with cord. Place fish in a greased large shallow baking pan. Mix cider and 2 tablespoons melted butter; brush over fish.
4. Bake at 375°F, brushing occasionally with cider mixture, 25 to 30 minutes, or until fish flakes easily when pierced with a fork. If additional browning is desired, place fish under broiler 3 to 5 minutes. Transfer to a heated platter and remove skewers and cord. Garnish platter with parsley.

Drunken Fish

6 TO 8
SERVINGS

1 whole red snapper or
  similar fish, or 5 pounds
  fish fillets
Flour, seasoned with salt and
  pepper
¼ cup oil
1 cup chopped onion
1 clove garlic, minced
6 fresh or dried ancho chilies
1½ cups canned tomatoes
2 tablespoons dried parsley
½ teaspoon oregano
½ teaspoon cumin (comino)
Salt and pepper
2 cups dry red wine
2 tablespoons capers

1. Dredge the fish with seasoned flour. Heat oil in a large skillet and brown fish on both sides. Remove fish from skillet and place in a shallow baking dish.
2. Add onion and garlic to oil remaining in skillet and cook until onion is soft, about 5 minutes.
3. Prepare chilies (see below); place in an electric blender and blend to a thick purée. Add to onion and garlic in skillet and cook about 5 minutes. Add tomatoes, parsley, oregano, and cumin. Bring to boiling, stirring constantly. Season to taste with salt and pepper. Stir in red wine and mix well.
4. Pour sauce over fish in baking dish.
5. Bake at 400°F about 30 minutes, or until fish flakes easily. Garnish with capers and serve.

How to prepare fresh chilies for cooking: Wash chilies and pat dry. If preparing a large number of big chilies, place on a broiler pan; place pan under broiler flame and roast chilies until well-blistered, turning to roast on all sides. For two or three chilies, or for the smaller varieties, roast in a small skillet over high heat until skins pop; chilies will be almost black. Remove from broiler or skillet and put into a plastic bag. Let stand a few minutes, then peel with sharp knife, beginning at the blossom end and working toward stem. Cut a slit in side of each chili and scoop out seeds and veins. If using for Chilies Rellenos, leave stems on to use as "handles." Otherwise, cut around stem with sharp knife and remove. *Note:* Wash hands with soap and water after handling fresh or dried chilies, as the small amount left on hands can burn if rubbed into eyes, or a small cut.

How to prepare dried chilies for cooking: Wash chilies and pat dry. Cut open and remove seeds, veins, and stems. Place in a small amount of water and boil until soft, about 10 minutes. Chop or blend as directed in recipe. Save water in which the chilies were boiled to use in whatever sauce you are preparing. Wash hands (see Note above).

How to use canned "Hot Peppers": These chilies may simply be chopped and used as they come from can or jar. To somewhat reduce the hotness, if desired, remove seeds and stems and rinse in cold water before chopping. Wash hands (see Note above).

Fish Stew

8 SERVINGS
(2 CUPS EACH)

3 pounds fish fillets,
  skinned*
5 medium tomatoes, peeled
  and chopped
3 carrots, chopped
1 large onion, thinly sliced
2 teaspoons salt
¼ teaspoon freshly ground
  pepper
2 garlic cloves, minced
1 teaspoon fennel seed,
  crushed
1 tablespoon minced orange
  peel
1 cup dry white wine
1 quart Fish Stock (page 70)

1. Cut fish into 1½-inch pieces. Set aside.
2. Simmer tomatoes, carrots, onion, salt, pepper, garlic, fennel, and orange peel in a mixture of wine and stock 15 minutes. Add fish to stock mixture; simmer covered until fish is tender and flakes with a fork (about 20 minutes).
3. Serve immediately in large shallow soup bowls.

*Flounder, haddock, cod, whitefish, halibut bass, or other fish can be used in this recipe. For maximum flavor and variety, select at least 3 kinds of fish.

Patio Crab Casserole

ABOUT
12 SERVINGS

¼ cup butter or margarine
2 cups chopped onion
1 pound frozen or 2 cans
  (7½ ounces each) Alaska
  king crab, drained and
  sliced
½ cup snipped parsley
2 tablespoons capers
2 tablespoons snipped chives
2 pimentos, diced
1½ cups corn muffin mix
⅛ teaspoon salt
1 egg, fork beaten
½ cup milk
1 cup cream-style golden
  corn
6 drops Tabasco
2 cups sour cream
1½ cups shredded extra
  sharp Cheddar cheese

1. Heat butter in a skillet. Add onion and cook until tender. Stir in crab, parsley, capers, chives, and pimentos; heat.
2. Meanwhile, stir corn muffin mix, salt, egg, milk, corn, and Tabasco until just moistened (batter should be lumpy). Turn into a greased shallow 3-quart dish and spread evenly to edges.
3. Spoon crab mixture and then sour cream over batter. Sprinkle cheese over all.
4. Bake at 400°F 25 to 30 minutes.
5. To serve, cut into squares.

Steamed Mussels in Wine Sauce

6 SERVINGS

2 pounds mussels
1 large onion, minced
1 large celery stak, minced
4 peppercorns
3 cups dry white wine
¼ cup butter (at room
  temperature)
1 tablespoon flour
1 teaspoon vinegar
1 tablespoon chopped parsley
1 garlic clove
Salt and pepper to taste

1. Scrub mussels well with a vegetable brush and rinse. Put into a kettle with onion, celery, peppercorns, and white wine. Cover and steam until they open, discarding any that are unopened.
2. Put mussels onto a deep platter. Cover and keep warm.
3. Strain liquid and simmer. Mix butter and flour together in a small bowl; stir into hot liquid. Add vinegar, parsley, garlic, salt, and pepper; continue to simmer until liquid is reduced by half.
4. To serve, pour sauce over mussels.

Creole Bouillabaisse

6 SERVINGS

1 pound red snapper fillets
1 pound redfish fillets
2 teaspoons minced parsley
1 teaspoon salt
¾ teaspoon thyme
½ teaspoon allspice
⅛ teaspoon pepper
2 bay leaves, finely crushed
1 clove garlic, finely minced
  or crushed in a garlic press
2 tablespoons olive oil
1 large onion, chopped
1 cup white wine
3 large ripe tomatoes, peeled
  and cut in ¼-inch slices
3 or 4 lemon slices
1 cup hot Fish Stock (see
  below) or hot water
¾ teaspoon salt
⅛ teaspoon pepper
Dash cayenne pepper
Pinch of saffron
6 slices buttered, toasted
  bread

1. Thoroughly rub into fish fillets a mixture of parsley, salt, thyme, allspice, pepper, bay leaf, and garlic. Set fillets aside.
2. Heat olive oil in a large skillet over low heat; add onion and fillets. Cover and cook over low heat 10 minutes, turning fillets once.
3. Remove fish fillets from skillet; set aside and keep warm. Pour wine into skillet, stirring well; add tomato slices and bring to boiling. Add lemon slices, hot fish stock, salt, pepper, and cayenne pepper. Simmer about 25 minutes, or until liquid is reduced by almost one half.
4. Add fish fillets to skillet and continue cooking 5 minutes longer.
5. Meanwhile, blend several tablespoons of the liquid in which the fish is cooking with saffron. When fish has cooked 5 minutes, spread saffron mixture over fillets. Remove fillets from liquid and place on buttered toast. Pour liquid over fish. Serve at once.

Fish Stock: Combine **1 quart water, 1 tablespoon salt, and 1 pound fish trimmings** (head, bones, skin, and tail) in a large saucepan. Cover and simmer 30 minutes. Strain liquid and use as directed.
ABOUT 1 QUART STOCK

Paella

8 TO 10
SERVINGS

1 cup olive or vegetable oil
1 broiler-fryer chicken (2
  pounds), cut in pieces
½ cup diced boiled ham or
  smoky sausage
1 tablespoon minced onion
2 cloves garlic, minced
2 ripe tomatoes, peeled and
  coarsely chopped
1½ teaspoons salt
1½ pounds fresh shrimp,
  shelled and deveined
12 small clams in shells,
  scrubbed
2 cups uncooked rice
1 quart hot water
1 cup fresh or frozen green
  peas
¼ cup coarsely chopped
  parsley
Few shreds saffron
1 rock lobster tail, cooked
  and meat cut in pieces
1 can or jar (7 ounces) whole
  pimentos

1. Heat oil in paellera or large skillet; cook chicken and ham about 10 minutes, turning chicken to brown on all sides. Add onion and garlic and cook 2 minutes. Add tomatoes, salt, shrimp, and clams; cover and cook 5 to 10 minutes, or until clam shells open. Remove clams and keep warm.
2. Add rice, water, peas, parsley, and saffron; mix well. Cover and cook, stirring occasionally, 25 minutes, or until rice is just tender. Mix in lobster, half of pimento, and the reserved clams in shells; heat until very hot. Serve garnished with remaining pimento.

Shrimp San Giusto

3 TO 4 SERVINGS

1 pound large uncooked
  shrimp
½ teaspoon salt
⅛ teaspoon pepper
1 bay leaf
3 tablespoons lemon juice
2½ cups water
1 bay leaf
1 thick slice onion
Pinch each salt, pepper,
  thyme, and oregano
2 tablespoons olive oil
1 tablespoon butter
½ cup finely chopped onion
1 clove garlic, finely chopped
1 teaspoon finely chopped
  parsley
Flour
⅓ cup dry white wine
1 large tomato, peeled,
  seeded, and chopped

1. Using scissors, cut the shells of the shrimp down middle of back; remove shells and set aside. Clean and devein shrimp.
2. Place cleaned shrimp in a bowl with salt, pepper, and a bay leaf; drizzle with lemon juice. Set shrimp aside to marinate 1 hour.
3. To make fish stock, place shrimp shells in a saucepan with water, a bay leaf, onion slice, salt, pepper, thyme, and oregano. Cover and simmer 30 minutes; strain.
4. Heat olive oil and butter in a skillet. Add chopped onion, garlic, and parsley; cook until soft. Coat marinated shrimp with flour, add to skillet with vegetables, and cook until lightly browned on both sides.
5. Add wine and simmer until it is almost evaporated. Stir in tomato and ½ cup or more of the strained fish stock. Simmer 15 to 20 minutes, or until the sauce is desired consistency.

African Rock Lobster en Casserole

6 SERVINGS

6 (3 ounces each) frozen
  South African rock lobster
  tails
¼ cup butter or margarine
¼ cup flour
2 cups chicken broth
2 egg yolks, fork beaten
⅓ cup half-and-half
2 to 3 teaspoons Worcestershire sauce
1 teaspoon dry mustard
  blended with about 1
  tablespoon cold water
1 or 2 packages (10 ounces
  each) frozen asparagus
  spears, cooked following
  package directions
1 package (8 ounces)
  spaghetti, cooked and
  drained
Parmesan-Romano cheese
¼ cup toasted slivered
  almonds

1. Drop frozen lobster tails into boiling salted water. Return to boiling and simmer 3 minutes.
2. Remove cooked lobster tails and place under running cold water until cool enough to handle. With scissors, cut along each edge of bony membrane on the underside of shell; remove meat.
3. Dice half of the meat and cut remainder into chunks; set aside.
4. Heat butter in a heavy saucepan; stir in flour. Cook until bubbly. Add broth gradually while blending thoroughly. Stirring constantly, bring rapidly to boiling and cook 1 to 2 minutes. Immediately blend about 3 tablespoonfuls into egg yolks and stir into the hot sauce. Cook 3 to 5 minutes, stirring constantly.
5. Blend in half-and-half, Worcestershire sauce, mustard, and diced lobster. Heat thoroughly.
6. Divide cooked asparagus equally among 6 individual casseroles. Spoon over spaghetti and hot lobster sauce. Generously shake cheese over all. Top with lobster chunks and almonds.

 ## Savory Outdoor Baked Fish

Scale and clean fish, leaving whole. Place fish on individual sheets of heavy-duty aluminum foil and brush with melted butter or oil. Sprinkle with salt and pepper and drizzle with lemon juice. Top each fish with a teaspoonful of chopped tomato or pimento and garnish with lemon slices. Bring foil up over fish and seal with a double fold. Seal ends. Place on grill over a medium-hot fire and cook 10 minutes on a side for a small 1- to 1½-pound fish, 15 minutes on a side for 2- to 3-pound fish, and about 20 minutes on a side for 4- to 5-pound fish. Open foil; if fish flakes easily when tested with a fork, it is done. Serve with juices from bottom of package.

Desserts

Indian Pudding

6 SERVINGS

3 cups milk
½ cup cornmeal
1 tablespoon butter or
margarine
½ cup light molasses
½ teaspoon salt
½ teaspoon ginger
1 cup cold milk

1. Scald 2½ cups milk in top of double boiler over boiling water.
2. Combine cornmeal and the remaining ½ cup milk. Add to scalded milk, stirring constantly. Cook about 25 minutes, stirring frequently.
3. Stir in butter, molasses, salt, and ginger.
4. Pour into a greased 1½-quart baking dish. Pour the 1 cup cold milk over pudding.
5. Set in a baking pan. Pour boiling water around dish to within 1 inch of top.
6. Bake, covered, at 300°F about 2 hours. Remove cover and bake an additional 1 hour. Serve warm or cold with **cream** or **ice cream.**

Brazilian Pudim Moka with Chocolate Sauce

8 SERVINGS

3 cups milk
1 cup half-and-half
5 tablespoons instant coffee
2 teaspoons grated orange
peel
4 eggs
1 egg yolk
½ cup sugar
½ teaspoon salt
1 teaspoon vanilla extract
Nutmeg
Chocolate sauce
Chopped Brazil nuts

1. Combine milk and half-and-half in top of a double boiler and heat over simmering water until scalded.
2. Add instant coffee and orange peel, stirring until coffee is dissolved. Remove from simmering water and set aside to cool (about 10 minutes).
3. Beat together eggs and egg yolk slightly. Blend in sugar and salt.
4. Gradually add coffee mixture, stirring constantly. Mix in vanilla extract. Strain through a fine sieve into eight 6-ounce custard cups. Sprinkle with nutmeg. Set cups in pan of hot water.
5. Bake, uncovered, at 325°F 25 to 30 minutes, or until a knife inserted in center of custard comes out clean.
6. Cool and chill. To serve, invert onto serving plates. Pour chocolate sauce over top and sprinkle with Brazil nuts.

Chocolate Custard

8 TO 10
SERVINGS

1 package (6 ounces)
semisweet chocolate pieces
3 tablespoons half-and-half
3 cups milk
3 eggs
1 teaspoon vanilla extract
⅓ cup sugar
¼ teaspoon salt

1. Melt ⅔ cup chocolate pieces with half-and-half in top of a double boiler over hot (not boiling) water. Stir until smooth; spoon about 1 tablespoon into each of 8 custard cups or 10 soufflé dishes. Spread evenly. Put cups into a shallow pan; set aside.
2. Scald milk. Melt remaining ⅓ cup chocolate pieces and, adding gradually, stir in scalded milk until blended.
3. Beat together eggs, vanilla extract, sugar, and salt. Gradually add milk mixture, stirring constantly. Pour into chocolate-lined cups.
4. Set pan with filled cups on oven rack and pour boiling water into pan to a depth of 1 inch.

5. Bake, uncovered, at 325°F 25 minutes, or until a knife inserted halfway between center and edge comes out clean.
6. Set cups on wire rack to cool slightly. Refrigerate and serve when thoroughly cooled. Unmold and, if desired, garnish with whipped cream rosettes.

Coconut Flan

6 SERVINGS

Caramel Topping:
½ cup granulated sugar
2 tablespoons water

Custard:
2 cups milk
4 eggs
¼ cup sugar
⅛ teaspoon salt
½ teaspoon vanilla extract
⅓ cup shredded or flaked
   coconut

1. For caramel topping, heat sugar and water in a small skillet, stirring constantly, until sugar melts and turns golden brown.
2. Pour syrup into a 1-quart baking dish or 6 custard cups, tipping to coat bottom and part way up sides. Set dish aside while preparing custard.
3. For custard, scald milk. Beat eggs; beat in sugar, salt, and vanilla extract. Gradually beat scalded milk into egg mixture. Strain into prepared baking dish or custard cups. Sprinkle top with coconut.
4. Place baking dish in pan containing hot water which comes at least 1 inch up sides of dish.
5. Bake at 325°F about 45 minutes for individual custard cups, or 1 hour for baking dish.

Carrot Cupcakes

ABOUT
16 CUPCAKES

1½ cups sifted enriched all-
   purpose flour
1 teaspoon baking powder
1 teaspoon baking soda
1 teaspoon ground cinnamon
½ teaspoon salt
1 cup sugar
¾ cup vegetable oil
2 eggs
1 cup grated raw carrots
½ cup chopped nuts

1. Blend flour, baking powder, baking soda, cinnamon, and salt. Set aside.
2. Combine sugar and oil in a bowl and beat thoroughly. Add eggs, one at a time, beating thoroughly after each addition. Mix in carrots. Add dry ingredients gradually, beating until blended. Mix in nuts.
3. Spoon into paper-baking-cup-lined muffin-pan wells.
4. Bake at 350°F 15 to 20 minutes.

Pecan Pie

ONE 9-INCH PIE

3 tablespoons butter or
   margarine
2 teaspoons vanilla extract
¾ cup sugar
3 eggs
½ cup chopped pecans
1 cup dark corn syrup
⅛ teaspoon salt
1 unbaked 9-inch pie shell
½ cup pecan halves

1. Cream butter with extract. Gradually add sugar, creaming well. Add eggs, one at a time, beating thoroughly after each addition.
2. Beat in chopped pecans, corn syrup, and salt. Turn into unbaked pie shell.
3. Bake at 450°F 10 minutes; reduce oven temperature to 350°F. Arrange pecan halves over top of filling. Bake 30 to 35 minutes, or until set. Cool on wire rack.

Black Bottom Pie

ONE
10-INCH PIE

½ cup sugar
4 teaspoons cornstarch
½ cup cold milk
1½ cups milk, scalded
4 egg yolks, slightly beaten
1 envelope unflavored gelatin
¼ cup cold water
1 tablespoon rum extract
1½ ounces (1½ square)
 unsweetened chocolate,
 melted and cooled
2 teaspoons vanilla extract
1 baked 10-inch pie shell
4 egg whites
¼ teaspoon salt
¼ teaspoon cream of tartar
½ cup sugar
1 cup heavy cream, whipped
½ ounce (½ square)
 unsweetened chocolate

1. Blend ½ cup sugar and cornstarch in a saucepan. Stir in the cold milk, then the scalded milk, adding gradually. Bring rapidly to boiling, stirring constantly. Cook 3 minutes.
2. Turn mixture into a double-boiler top and set over boiling water. Vigorously stir about 3 tablespoons of hot mixture into egg yolks. Immediately blend into mixture in double boiler. Cook over simmering water, stirring constantly, 3 to 5 minutes, or until mixture coats a metal spoon. Remove double-boiler top from hot water immediately.
3. Soften gelatin in the cold water. Remove 1 cup of the cooked filling and set aside. Immediately stir softened gelatin into mixture in double boiler until completely dissolved. Cool until mixture sets slightly. Blend in rum extract.
4. Blend the melted chocolate and vanilla extract into the 1 cup reserved filling. Cool completely; turn into the baked pie shell, spreading evenly over bottom. Chill until set.
5. Beat egg whites with salt until frothy. Add cream of tartar and beat slightly. Gradually add remaining ½ cup sugar, beating well after each addition; continue beating until stiff peaks are formed. Spread over gelatin mixture and gently fold together. Turn onto chocolate filling in pie shell. Chill until firm.
6. Spread whipped cream over pie, swirling for a decorative effect. Top with chocolate curls shaved from the ½ ounces unsweetened chocolate. Chill until ready to serve.

Strawberry Shortcake

ABOUT
6 SERVINGS

1¾ cups all-purpose flour
2 tablespoons sugar
1 tablespoon baking powder
½ teaspoon salt
½ cup lard, chilled
¾ cup milk
Sweetened sliced ripe
 strawberries

1. Blend the flour, sugar, baking powder, and salt in a bowl. Cut in the lard with a pastry blender or two knives until particles are about the size of coarse cornmeal. Make a well in the center and add milk all at one time. Stir with a fork 20 to 30 strokes.
2. Turn dough out onto a lightly floured surface and shape it into a ball. Knead lightly with the fingertips about 15 times.
3. Divide dough into halves. Roll each half about ¼ inch thick to fit an 8-inch layer cake pan. Place one round of dough in pan and brush with **melted butter or margarine.** Cover with the other round. Brush top with **milk.**
4. Bake at 425°F 15 to 18 minutes, or until top is delicately browned.
5. Split shortcake while hot and spread with **butter or margarine.** Arrange half of the strawberry slices over bottom layer. Spoon **whipped dessert topping, sour cream,** or **sweetened whipped cream** over berries. Cover with top layer and arrange remaining berries over it. Spoon additional topping over all.

Note: **Orange or lemon marmalade** or **strawberry jam** may be thinly spread over layers before adding strawberries and topping.

Peach Shortcake: Follow recipe for Strawberry Shortcake. Substitute sweetened **fresh peach slices** for strawberries.

Sunshine Shortcake: Follow recipe for Strawberry Shortcake. Substitute **orange sections,** sliced **banana,** and **confectioners' sugar** for strawberries.

Blueberry Orange Cheese Cake

ONE 9-INCH
CHEESE CAKE

1½ cups graham cracker
  crumbs
2 tablespoons sugar
½ teaspoon cinnamon
½ teaspoon nutmeg
6 tablespoons butter, melted
4 cups cream-style cottage
  cheese
Heavy cream
6 eggs
1½ cups sugar
½ cup all-purpose flour
3 tablespoons thawed frozen
  orange juice concentrate
1 teaspoon vanilla extract
⅛ teaspoon salt
1 cup sour cream
2 tablespoons confectioners'
  sugar
1 cup dry-pack frozen
  blueberries, thawed

1. Set out a 9-inch springform pan.
2. To prepare crust, combine graham cracker crumbs, sugar, cinnamon and nutmeg in a bowl.
3. Stir in butter.
4. Press the mixture on bottom and about three-fourths up sides of the springform pan. Chill crust while preparing the filling.
5. Drain cottage cheese (reserving the cream), press through a coarse sieve and set aside.
6. Measure reserved cream in a measuring cup for liquids and fill to 1-cup level with heavy cream.
7. In a large mixing bowl, beat eggs until very thick.
8. Add sugar, beating until light and fluffy.
9. Blend in the sieved cottage cheese, the cream and flour, orange juice concentrate, vanilla extract, and salt. Mix well and turn filling into crumb-lined pan.
10. Bake at 350°F oven 1 hour and 10 to 20 minutes. (Cheese cake is done when a metal knife inserted in center comes out clean.)
11. While cake is baking, prepare topping. Combine sour cream, confectioners' sugar and blueberries in a small bowl.
12. When cake tests done, turn off heat. Open oven door and gently spread cake with topping mixture. Cool in oven until cake is of room temperature. Chill.

Note: Syrup-pack canned or frozen blueberries, drained, may be used in topping.

Date Spice Cake

ONE 9-INCH
SQUARE CAKE

2¼ cups sifted enriched all-
  purpose flour
2 teaspoons baking powder
¼ teaspoon baking soda
½ teaspoon salt
2 teaspoons ground nutmeg
2 teaspoons ground ginger
⅔ cup shortening
1 teaspoon grated orange
  peel
1 teaspoon grated lemon peel
1 cup sugar
2 eggs
1 cup buttermilk
1 cup chopped dates

1. Grease a 9x9x2-inch pan. Line with waxed paper cut to fit bottom; grease paper. Set aside.
2. Blend flour, baking powder, baking soda, salt, nutmeg, and ginger.
3. Beat shortening with orange and lemon peels. Add sugar gradually, creaming until fluffy after each addition.
4. Add eggs, one at a time, beating thoroughly after each addition.
5. Beating only until smooth after each addition, alternately add dry ingredients in fourths and buttermilk in thirds to creamed mixture. Mix in dates. Turn batter into prepared pan.
6. Bake at 350°F about 45 minutes.
7. Remove from oven. Cool 5 to 10 minutes in pan on wire rack. Remove cake from pan and peel off paper; cool cake on rack.

Raisin-Nut Spice Cake

1 LARGE CAKE;
16 SERVINGS

3 cups sifted cake flour
2 teaspoons baking powder
1 teaspoon baking soda
½ teaspoon cinnamon
½ teaspoon nutmeg
¼ teaspoon ginger
¼ teaspoon salt
1 can or bottle (12 ounces) beer
1 cup raisins (5 ounces)
¾ cup butter or margarine
1 cup sugar
½ cup molasses
2 eggs
¾ cup chopped nuts (3 ounces)
Glaze

1. Sift dry ingredients together. Set aside.
2. Heat beer and raisins to simmering; let stand about 15 minutes to plump.
3. Cream butter and sugar until light and fluffy; add molasses.
4. Add eggs, one at a time, beating well after each addition.
5. Add dry ingredients alternately in thirds with beer drained from raisins, beating just until well blended. Stir in raisins and nuts.
6. Turn into a well-greased and floured 10-inch Bundt pan or angel food cake pan (nonstick pan preferred).
8. Let stand in pan about 10 minutes; invert onto cake rack. Cool. Cover with foil or store in airtight container. Cake slices better if made a day in advance.
9. Prepare a glaze by thinning **1 cup sifted confectioners' sugar** with **beer** or **milk**. Drizzle over cake shortly before serving.

Glazed Apple Tart in Wheat Germ Crust

ONE
10-INCH TART

Wheat Germ Crust (below)
8 medium apples
1 cup red port
1 cup water
⅓ cup honey
2 tablespoons lemon juice
⅛ teaspoon salt
3 drops red food coloring
1 package (8 ounces) cream cheese
1 tablespoon half-and-half
1 tablespoon honey
1½ tablespoons cornstarch

1. Prepare crust and set aside to cool.
2. Pare, core, and cut apples into eighths to make 2 quarts.
3. Combine port, water, ⅓ cup honey, lemon juice, salt, and food coloring in large skillet with a cover. Add half the apples in single layer, cover, and cook slowly about 5 minutes, until apples are barely tender. Remove apples with slotted spoon and arrange in a single layer in a shallow pan. Cook remaining apples in same manner. Chill apples, saving cooking liquid for glaze.
4. Beat cream cheese with half-and-half and 1 tablespoon honey. Spread in even layer over bottom of cooled crust, saving about ¼ cup for decoration on top of tart, if desired.
5. Arrange apples over cheese.
6. Boil syrup from cooking apples down to 1 cup.
7. Mix cornstarch with 1½ tablespoons cold water. Stir into syrup, and cook, stirring, until mixture clears and thickens. Set pan in cold water, and cool quickly to room temperature. Spoon carefully over apples.
8. Chill until glaze is set before cutting.

Wheat Germ Crust

ONE
10-INCH CRUST

1½ cups sifted all-purpose flour
3 tablespoons packed brown sugar
¾ teaspoon salt
⅛ teaspoon cinnamon
6 tablespoons shortening
2 tablespoons butter
2 tablespoons milk (about)

1. Combine flour, wheat germ, brown sugar, salt, and cinnamon in mixing bowl.
2. Cut in shortening and butter as for pie crust.
3. Sprinkle with just enough milk to make dough stick together.
4. Press dough against bottom and up sides of 10-inch spring-form pan to make shell 1¾ inches deep. Prick bottom. Set on baking sheet.
5. Bake at 375°F on lowest shelf of oven for about 20 minutes, or until golden.

Cherry-Pineapple Cobbler

8 SERVINGS

1 can (21 ounces) cherry pie
filling
1 can (13¼ ounces) pineapple tidbits, drained
¼ teaspoon allspice
3 tablespoons honey
1 egg, slightly beaten
½ cup sour cream
1½ cups unflavored croutons

1. Combine cherry pie filling, pineapple tidbits, allspice, and 1 tablespoon honey. Put into a 1½-quart baking dish.
2. Blend egg, sour cream, and remaining 2 tablespoons honey. Stir in croutons. Spoon over cherry-pineapple mixture.
3. Bake, uncovered, at 375°F 30 minutes, or until heated through. If desired, top with ice cream.

Spicy Peach Cobbler

6 SERVINGS

1 can (29 ounces) sliced
peaches, drained; reserve 1
cup syrup
½ cup firmly packed brown
sugar
2 tablespoons cornstarch
⅛ teaspoon salt
⅛ teaspoon ground
cinnamon
⅛ teaspoon ground cloves
2 tablespoons cider vinegar
1 tablespoon butter or
margarine
1 cup all-purpose biscuit mix
½ cup finely shredded sharp
Cheddar cheese
2 tablespoons butter or
margarine, melted
¼ cup milk

1. Put drained peaches into a shallow 1-quart baking dish. Set aside.
2. Mix brown sugar, cornstarch, salt, cinnamon, and cloves in a saucepan. Blend in reserved peach syrup and vinegar; add 1 tablespoon butter. Bring mixture to boiling, stirring frequently; cook until thickened, about 10 minutes. Pour over peaches and set in a 400°F oven.
3. Combine biscuit mix and cheese. Stir in melted butter and milk to form a soft dough. Remove dish from oven and drop dough by heaping tablespoonfuls on top of hot peaches.
4. Return to oven and bake 20 minutes, or until crust is golden brown. Serve warm.

Rosy Rhubarb Swirls

12 SERVINGS

1½ cups sugar
1¼ cups water
⅓ cup red cinnamon candies
2 or 3 drops red food
coloring
2¼ cups all-purpose flour
4 teaspoons baking powder
½ teaspoon salt
⅔ cup milk
⅓ cup half-and-half
3 cups finely diced fresh
rhubarb (if tender do not
peel)

1. Put sugar, water, and cinnamon candies into a saucepan. Stirring occasionally, cook over medium heat until candies are melted and mixture forms a thin syrup (about 10 minutes). Stir in food coloring.
2. Meanwhile, sift together into a bowl the flour, baking powder, and salt. Add a mixture of milk and half-and-half and stir with a fork only until dry ingredients are moistened. Turn onto a floured surface and knead lightly about 10 times with fingertips.
3. Roll dough into a 13x11x¼-inch rectangle. Spoon rhubarb evenly over dough. Beginning with longer side, roll dough and seal edges. Cut crosswise into 12 slices.
4. Pour syrup into a shallow baking dish and arrange rolls, cut side up, in syrup. Sprinkle with additional sugar (¼ to ⅓ cup) and top each roll with a small piece of **butter**.
5. Bake, uncovered, at 400°F 25 to 30 minutes. Serve warm with **half-and-half**.

Index

WEIGHTS AND MEASURES

English System

LINEAR MEASURE
12 inches	= 1 foot
3 feet	= 1 yard
5½ yards	= 1 rod
40 rods	= 1 furlong
8 furlongs (5280 feet)	= 1 statute mile

MARINERS' MEASURE
6 feet	= 1 fathom
1000 fathoms (approx.)	= 1 nautical mile
3 nautical miles	= 1 league

SQUARE MEASURE
144 square inches	= 1 square foot
9 square feet	= 1 square yard
30¼ square yards	= 1 square rod
160 square rods	= 1 acre
640 acres	= 1 square mile

CUBIC MEASURE
1728 cubic inches	= 1 cubic foot
27 cubic feet	= 1 cubic yard

SURVEYORS' MEASURE
7.92 inches	= 1 link
100 links	= 1 chain

LIQUID MEASURE
4 gills	= 1 pint
2 pints	= 1 quart
4 quarts	= 1 gallon
31½ gallons	= 1 barrel
2 barrels	= 1 hogshead

APOTHECARIES' FLUID MEASURE
60 minims	= 1 fluid dram
8 fluid drams	= 1 fluid ounce
16 fluid ounces	= 1 pint
2 pints	= 1 quart
4 quarts	= 1 gallon

DRY MEASURE
2 pints	= 1 quart
8 quarts	= 1 peck
4 pecks	= 1 bushel

WOOD MEASURE
16 cubic feet	= 1 cord foot
8 cord feet	= 1 cord

TIME MEASURE
60 seconds	= 1 minute
60 minutes	= 1 hour
24 hours	= 1 day
7 days	= 1 week
4 weeks (28 to 31 days)	= 1 month
12 months (365-366 days)	= 1 year
100 years	= 1 century

ANGULAR AND CIRCULAR MEASURE
60 seconds	= 1 minute
60 minutes	= 1 degree
90 degrees	= 1 right angle
180 degrees	= 1 straight angle
360 degrees	= 1 circle

TROY WEIGHT
24 grains	= 1 pennyweight
20 pennyweights	= 1 ounce
12 ounces	= 1 pound

AVOIRDUPOIS WEIGHT
$27\frac{11}{32}$ grains	= 1 dram
16 drams	= 1 ounce
16 ounces	= 1 pound
100 pounds	= 1 short hundredweight
20 short hundredweight	= 1 short ton

APOTHECARIES' WEIGHT
20 grains	= 1 scruple
3 scruples	= 1 dram
8 drams	= 1 ounce
12 ounces	= 1 pound

Metric System

LINEAR MEASURE
10 millimeters	= 1 centimeter
10 centimeters	= 1 decimeter
10 decimeters	= 1 meter
10 meters	= 1 decameter
10 decameters	= 1 hectometer
10 hectometers	= 1 kilometer

SQUARE MEASURE
100 sq. millimeters	= 1 sq. centimeter
100 sq. centimeters	= 1 sq. decimeter
100 sq. decimeters	= 1 sq. meter
100 sq. meters	= 1 sq. decameter
100 sq. decameters	= 1 sq. hectometer
100 sq. hectometers	= 1 sq. kilometer

CUBIC MEASURE
1000 cu. millimeters	= 1 cu. centimeter
1000 cu. centimeters	= 1 cu. decimeter
1000 cu. decimeters	= 1 cu. meter

LIQUID MEASURE
10 milliliters	= 1 centiliter
10 centiliters	= 1 deciliter
10 deciliters	= 1 liter
10 liters	= 1 decaliter
10 decaliters	= 1 hectoliter
10 hectoliters	= 1 kiloliter

WEIGHTS
10 milligrams	= 1 centigram
10 centigrams	= 1 decigram
10 decigrams	= 1 gram
10 grams	= 1 decagram
10 decagrams	= 1 hectogram
10 hectograms	= 1 kilogram
100 kilograms	= 1 quintal
10 quintals	= 1 ton

Metric and English Equivalents

LINEAR MEASURE
English Unit	Metric Unit
1 inch =	25.4 millimeters
	2.54 centimeters
1 foot =	30.48 centimeters
	3.048 decimeters
	0.3048 meter
1 yard =	0.9144 meter
1 mile =	1609.3 meters
	1.6093 kilometers
0.03937 inch	= 1 millimeter
0.3937 inch	= 1 centimeter
3.937 inches	= 1 decimeter
39.37 inches	
3.2808 feet	= 1 meter
1.0936 yards	
3280.8 feet	
1093.6 yards	= 1 kilometer
0.62137 mile	

LIQUID MEASURE
English Unit	Metric Unit
1 fluid ounce =	29.573 milliliters
1 quart =	9.4635 deciliters
	0.94635 liter
1 gallon =	3.7854 liters
0.033814 fluid ounce	= 1 milliliter
3.3814 fluid ounces	= 1 deciliter
33.814 fluid ounces	
1.0567 quarts	= 1 liter
0.26417 gallon	

SQUARE MEASURE
English Unit	Metric Unit
1 square inch =	645.16 square millimeters
	6.4516 square centimeters
1 square foot =	929.03 square centimeters
	9.2903 square decimeters
	0.092903 square meter
1 square yard =	0.83613 square meter
1 square mile =	2.5900 square kilometers
0.0015500 square inch	= 1 square millimeter
0.15500 square inch	= 1 square centimeter
15.500 square inches	= 1 square decimeter
0.10764 square foot	
1.1960 square yards	= 1 square meter
0.38608 square mile	= 1 square kilometer

CUBIC MEASURE
English Unit	Metric Unit
1 cubic inch =	16.387 cubic centimeters
	0.016387 liter
1 cubic foot =	0.028317 cubic meter
1 cubic yard =	0.76455 cubic meter
1 cubic mile =	4.16818 cubic kilometers
0.061023 cubic inch	= 1 cubic centimeter
61.023 cubic inches	= 1 cubic decimeter
35.315 cubic feet	= 1 cubic meter
1.3079 cubic yards	
0.23990 cubic mile	= 1 cubic kilometer

DRY MEASURE
English Unit	Metric Unit
1 quart =	1.1012 liters
1 peck =	8.8098 liters
1 bushel =	35.239 liters
0.90808 quart	
0.11351 peck	= 1 liter
0.028378 bushel	

WEIGHTS
English Unit	Metric Unit
1 grain	= 0.064799 gram
1 avoirdupois ounce	= 28.350 grams
1 troy ounce	= 31.103 grams
1 avoirdupois pound	= 0.45359 kilogram
1 troy pound	= 0.37324 kilogram
1 short ton (0.8929 long ton)	= 907.18 kilograms
	0.90718 metric ton
1 long ton (1.1200 short tons)	= 1016.0 kilograms
	1.0160 metric tons
15.432 grains	
0.035274 avoirdupois ounce	= 1 gram
0.032151 troy ounce	
2.2046 avoirdupois pounds	= 1 kilogram
0.98421 long ton	= 1 metric ton
1.1023 short tons	